MARIVAUX AND MOLIERE

A COMPARISON

BY

ALFRED CISMARU

1977
TEXAS TECH PRESS
LUBBOCK, TEXAS

Texas Tech Press, Lubbock, Texas, 79409, U.S.A.
Copyright 1977 by Texas Tech University
Printed in the United States of America

This book is dedicated

to

Claud and David

ACKNOWLEDGMENTS

Limited parts of this book have appeared in a number of periodicals. Permission to reprint certain brief passages gratefully is acknowledged to the following: *The French Review* for "Agnès and Angélique: An Attempt to Settle the Relationship," and "*Les Sincères* and *Le Misanthrope*"; *Cithara* for "*La Princesse d'Elide* in Marivaux's Theatre," "Marivaux's Religious Characters," and "Marivaux's *Les Fausses confidences*"; *Kentucky Foreign Language Quarterly* for "*Le Tartuffe* in Marivaux's Works"; *Kentucky Romance Quarterly* for "The Moliéresque Origins of *Les Fausses confidences*"; *South Central Bulletin Studies* for "Molière's Influence on Marivaux's *Les Serments indiscrets*"; and *South Atlantic Bulletin* for "Molière's Influence on Marivaux's *Le Père prudent et équitable*."

CONTENTS

PREFACE

When Pierre Carlet de Marivaux died on 12 February 1763, a poor man and an almost forgotten playwright, few were those acquaintances, friends, and critics who were willing to spend their time acknowledging the event. His not-too-sporadic successes on the stage, and his occasionally immense popularity with certain plays notwithstanding, by 1763 an almost total eclipse of his fame had occurred. Marivaux's death was announced in only three lines in the *Gazette de France*, was ignored by the *Mercure de France*, and hardly was mentioned in the memoirs of the period. One of his closest friends, for example, Charles S. Favart, whose own wife had made her debut as Marianne in *L'Epreuve*, and who, not too long before, had called on Marivaux in connection with a proposed private performance of *Les Serments indiscrets*, did not even mention the playwright's death. Yet, he often took notice of the passing of other writers: he devoted five pages to the death of Crébillon the Elder in July 1762, an author almost forgotten today, and in December 1763 he recorded the passing of the poet Victor Roy, an almost unknown during his entire lifetime.[1]

Moreover and in spite of a long-standing tradition, which requires that a new academician praise his predecessor upon accepting his seat, Abbé Radonvilliers said very little about the deceased, and likewise Cardinal de Luyens, Secretary of the Academy, failed to recall the Immortal who had just passed away. Of course, Voltaire's famous remark (repeated persistently in the salons of the time) that Marivaux spent his time weighing flies' eggs in scales made of spider webs, had taken its toll, and in view of Voltaire's unequaled success in crushing his enemies (it will be recalled that in 1742, Marivaux and Voltaire were candidates for a vacant seat in the Academy and that Marivaux had won), it is hardly a surprise that even former friends of the playwright deserted him just before and after his death. Abbé Joseph de La Porte's comments, for example, followed the not too subtle and somewhat perverse procedure of praising mildly the author in one sentence or in one paragraph, and in the next diminishing or totally obliterating the merit previously stated. Thus, he admitted:

Cet auteur, voyant que ses prédécesseurs avaient épuisé tous les sujets des comédies de caractère, s'est livré à la composition des pièces d'intrigue; et dans ce genre, qui peut être varié à l'infini, ne voulant avoir d'autre modèle que lui-même, il s'est frayé une route nouvelle. Il a imaginé d'introduire la métaphysique sur la scène, et d'analyser le coeur humain. . . . [But, the critic goes on] Ainsi le canevas de ses comédies n'est-il ordinairement qu'une petite

---

[1]See his letters to the Comte de Durazzo in *Mémoires et correspondances littéraires, dramatiques et anecdotiques* (Paris: Collin, 1808), 81, 123.

toile fort légère. . . . Concluez donc que les défauts qu'on remarque dans les oeuvres dramatiques de Marivaux, ne viennent que d'une surabondance d'esprit, qui fait tort à la délicatesse de son goût: tels sont ces dialogues si spirituels et si ennuyeux, entre des interlocuteurs qui regorgent d'esprit et manquent de sens, qui épuisent une idée et jouent sur le mot, pour égayer ridiculement un tissu de scènes métaphysiques; ces tristes analyses du sentiment, qui peignent ni les moeurs, ni le ridicule des hommes; ces réflexions subtiles, qui suffoquent les spectateurs; ces métaphores, toujours neuves à la vérité, mais souvent hardies, quelquefois hasardées; ces expressions détournées, qui n'ont de piquant que la singularité de leur association.[2]

Equally perfidious were the comments of Président Hénault, who, although a friend of Marivaux for several decades, was, in 1763, most unappreciative of the writer's works. "C'était l'anatomiste du coeur," he said, but then added: "il se plaisait peut-être un peu trop aux détails; mais il n'ennuyait pas, il aurait prouvé la divisibilité de l'âme à l'infini."[3] On the other hand, the German philosopher Grimm, who reflected the opinions of Voltaire, Diderot, and the other *philosophes* of the time, criticized without eulogizing, in a straightforward, if inimical manner:

S'il est vrai que ses romans ont été les modèles des romans de Richardson et de Fielding, on peut dire que, pour la première fois, un mauvais original a fait faire des copies admirables. Il a eu parmi nous la destinée d'une jolie femme [Emile Faguet, in his criticism, used to speak of the writer as *La Comtesse de Marivaux*], et qui n'est que cela, c'est-à-dire un printemps fort brillant, un automne et un hiver des plus durs et des plus tristes. Le souffle vigoureux de la philosophie a renversé depuis une quinzaine d'années toutes ces réputations étayées sur des roseaux.[4]

Today, however, Marivaux's popularity is widespread and attested in a variety of ways. After World War II, his plays began to be presented as often, if not more so, than those of other, more established seventeenth and eighteenth-century dramatists by the Comédie Francaise and other French theaters, both in the Capital and outside of it. In the 1950's and 1960's, no French theatrical group that traveled abroad failed to include on its repertory some Marivaux comedy. In addition, a veritable deluge of critical works, varying from articles to multivolumed studies, have been published by commentators who discovered or rediscovered the eighteenth-century playwright. Noteworthy in such affluent activity is the comparatively great number of articles and books in English that have appeared since World War II. Even a cursory look at the biblio-

[2]Joseph de La Porte, *L'Observateur littéraire* (Paris: Lambert, 1759), 1, 91.
[3]Président Hénault, *Mémoires du Président Hénault écrits par lui-même* (Paris: Dentu, 1885), 1, 411.
[4]Grimm, Diderot, Raynal, Meister, *Correspondance littéraire philosophique et critique* (Paris: Garnier, 1877), 5, 236.

graphical entries at the end of the present study should suffice to prove
this point.

In spite of the pejorative meaning of the word *marivaudage*, the
dramatist, it seems, benefited from the passing of time, which acted, in
his case, as a fortifying and maturing agent. Although the reception
accorded to him immediately after his death, in the nineteenth century,
and prior to 1945, was, at best, sporadic, the public and responding
critics were later eager to view plays that had no pretention at profound
metaphysics, did not attempt to solve the world's political problems,
and that, moreover, fell only painfully within categories or more established literary schools. Apparently, audiences exposed for years to the
propaganda of *isms* became increasingly alert to the complexities of the
heart that Marivaux attempted to analyze. His analysis, light, unscien-
tific, and devoid of bombastic conclusions, found almost universal
acclaim among audiences, which, after World War II, realized that
domestic and personal problems surpassed in importance those artificial entanglements and complexities created by would-be-philosophers
and, worse still, self-centered politicians. Within such an atmosphere,
it is no surprise that the work of a writer like Samuel Beckett, who had
declined to take sides publicly in World War II, could prosper
nevertheless and attain the acceptability that it enjoyed for many years.
In fact, Beckett's personages, like those of Ionesco and other famous
contemporary dramatists who refused to become involved in the more
pompous and less effective work of teachers, philosophers, men of
science, and politicians, are closer to the individual theatergoer with
whom they share the day-to-day struggles between loyalty and infidelity, boredom and solitude, and fears and aridity of heart.

At once classic and contemporary, the plays of Marivaux have
attained, then, a popularity that is both deserved and explainable:
deserved because the playwright contributed immensely to what he
called *la science du coeur humain*, that is, to that mature awareness of
the realities of personal relations to which the writer may contribute by
his representations of them; and explainable, as we have seen, in terms
of the particular time in history in which the revival of his plays took
place. Whereas his own contemporaries, for the most part, refused to
open their minds to the importance of his analysis of the heart, and
maintained that, as a dramatist, he wrote the same play over and over
again, the twentieth-century public, on the contrary, appears to have
accepted Marivaux's own defense as reported by d'Alembert.

Dans mes pièces, dit-il, c'est tantôt un amour ignoré des deux amants, tantôt un
amour qu'ils sentent et qu'ils veulent se cacher l'un à l'autre, tantôt un amour
timide, qui n'ose se déclarer; tantôt enfin un amour incertain et comme indécis,
un amour à demi né, pour ainsi dire, dont ils se doutent sans être bien sûrs, et

qu'ils épient au-dedans d'eux-mêmes avant de lui laisser prendre l'essor. Où est
en cela toute cette ressemblance qu'on ne cesse de m'objecter? Il n'en est rien, et
je n'y vois que la petitesse de certains rivaux jaloux et qui se plaisent à embêter les
gens.[5]

Some two centuries after his death, Marivaux can be seen both as a
national and an international wonder. In a Sunday morning talk with
subscribers of the Théâtre National Populaire, following his re-creation
of *L'Heureux stratagème,* when Jean Vilar described him publicly as
"an author of the mid-twentieth century," he did not exaggerate: in the
course of that season (1959-1960), spectators in France were exposed
to no fewer than twelve Marivaux plays. This number is particularly
astonishing if one recalls that the record for plays of one writer
produced in the course of a single season previously had been six,
belonging to the contemporary Jean Anouilh. Marivaux as an international *article de consommation* in the Western Hemisphere is old news
dating back some two decades; more recently, however, successful
presentations of his plays in the Near and Far East, and in such
otherwise propaganda-oriented countries as those of the Iron Curtain,
including the Soviet Union, have added an unexpected measure of
vitality to the eighteenth-century dramatist and his work. In fact, the
position of Marivaux is indeed extraordinary today: on the one hand, he
enjoys the prestige of a classic and elicits intense scholarly investiga-
tion in the universities; on the other, like a *new* playwright, he is being
discovered from time to time in various parts of the world, and, as the
living author that he is, he also inspires broader popularizations of his
work that have been received well inasmuch as they answer the desire
of a growing public to know more. As one recent critic has put it,
"Voltaire . . . had chosen to forget that flies' eggs are worth weighing
too, that weighing them is no easy matter, and that few artists are
dextrous enough to make scales, or anything else, of gossamer. While
Voltaire's own plays are shelved, while the tough Regnard is eclipsed,
and while even Beaumarchais must be propped up by Mozart and
Rossini, Marivaux seems as firmly settled in the French pantheon, a
place of no easy admission, as Molière himself. This is, with a vengeance, the Triumph of Gossamer."[6]

Yet, as the following chapter will attempt to show, for all the
attention bestowed upon him, there is one important aspect of

    [5]Jean le Rond d'Alembert, "Eloge de Marivaux," pp. 1, xxxii, in *Marivaux Théâtre,* Bernard
Dort, ed. (Paris: Le Club Français du Livre, 1961).
    [6]Oscar Mandel, *Seven Comedies by Marivaux* (Ithaca, New York: Cornell University Press,
1968), 7.

Marivaux's work that remains virtually untapped: that is, the
playwright's relationship with his great predecessor, Molière. [7]

---

[7] I have attempted sporadic analyses of this relationship in a number of articles: "Agnès and
Angélique: An Attempt to Settle the Relationship," *The French Review*, 35(April 1962):472-477;
"*La Princesse d'Elide* in Marivaux's Theatre," *Cithara*, 3(November 1963):15-23; "*Le Tartuffe* in
Marivaux's Works," *Kentucky Foreign Language Quarterly*, 12(Summer 1965):142-154;
"Marivaux's *Les Fausses confidences*," *Cithara*, 7(November 1967):67-73; "The Moliéresque
Origins of *Les Fausses confidences*," *Kentucky Romance Quarterly*, 15(Spring 1968):223-229; "*Les
Sincères* and *Le Misanthrope*," *The French Review*, 42(May 1969):865-870; "Molière's Influence
on Marivaux's *Les Serments indiscrets*," *South Central Bulletin Studies*, 32(Winter 1972):188-199;
and "Molière's Influence on Marivaux's *Le Père prudent et équitable*," *South Atlantic Bulletin*,
37(Spring 1973):23-28.

MARIVAUX AND MOLIERE

INTRODUCTION

In the enormous bibliography devoted to Marivaux, there are far fewer studies of his theater than of other aspects of the writer and his work. Many commentators have written about Marivaux the man, the novelist, the moralist, the philosopher, but relatively fewer have discussed thoroughly his theater. The first English popularization of the plays of the eighteenth-century dramatist was that of Kenneth N. McKee, *The Theater of Marivaux*, which treated each play as a unit and studied the playwright's entire theater in chronological order.[1] A later, more complete work going deeper into the historical and biographical background of each comedy appeared in Canada and was authored by E. J. H. Greene.[2]

French literary historians have touched often on Marivaux's theater: Gustave Larroumet's book, a good source on Marivaux, dates back, however, to 1881; Emile Gossot, in his *Marivaux moraliste*, is more interested in Marivaux's moralizing, the theater being discussed as only one facet of the writer; Jean Fleury's *Marivaux et le marivaudage* is concerned with Marivaux's work as a whole, and with the meaning of the second noun in its title; the same is true of Frédéric Deloffre's *Marivaux et le marivaudage*, although the book does contain one of the most complete bibliographies to date on Marivaux; Gaston Deschamps' *Marivaux* and Eugene Meyer's work of the same title are not concerned primarily with the writer's comedies; nor is Marcel Arland's *Marivaux*, which devotes only one third of its pages to the author's plays.

Most of the above books mention some of the sources of Marivaux. None, however, treats the subject of sources in detail, and none has analyzed systematically the relationship between Molière's theater and that of Marivaux. This lacuna appears to be in dire need of filling, especially in view of the contradictory statements, and of the affirmations and denials that have been advanced with respect to the influence of the seventeenth-century writer on Marivaux. It would be cumbersome to enumerate all of these, but a few are representative and will be cited below.

The opening sentences of Kenneth N. McKee's book state: "Marivaux was the most original French dramatist of the eighteenth century. In an age when leading dramatists, writing for the Théâtre Français, blindly followed the Molière tradition, Marivaux, writing principally for the Théâtre Italien and sometimes for the Théâtre Français, dared to be different. In fact, he repudiated Molière so

---

[1]Kenneth N. McKee, *The Theater of Marivaux* (New York: New York University Press, 1958).
[2]E. J. H. Greene, *Marivaux* (Toronto: University of Toronto Press, 1965).

openly that he drew the wrath of critics and public alike."[3] This is, of course, in line with what D'Alembert had reported of Marivaux. " 'J' aime mieux, disait Marivaux, être humblement assis sur le dernier banc dans la petite troupe des auteurs originaux, qu'orgueilleusement placé à la première ligne dans le nombreux bétail des singes littéraires.' " And D'Alembert commented: "Il avait le malheur de ne pas estimer beaucoup Molière, et le malheur plus grand de ne pas s'en cacher. Il ne craignait pas même, quand on le mettait à son aise sur cet article, d'avouer naïvement qu'il ne se croyait pas inférieur à ce grand peintre de la nature."[4] And, as a matter of fact, the critics for *Le Mercure de France*, when reviewing the plays of Marivaux in the 1720's and 1730's, made no mention of any possible *moliéresque* influence. It is curious that, close as they were to the theater of Molière, they failed to indicate any relationship between the seventeenth-century writer and Marivaux.

On the other hand, Molière specialists have made sweeping and even derogatory statements concerning the extended influence of Molière on Marivaux. Ferdinand Brunetière wrote, "Marivaux a voulu refaire telles et telles pièces de Molière, et non pas *Le Sicilien* ou *Le Mariage forcé*, mais *L'Ecole des femmes* dans son *Ecole des mères* et *Le Misanthrope* dans *Les Sincères*."[5] Other critics of Molière have expressed similar comments. For example, in speaking of the *surprise* plays of Marivaux, Maurice Donnay asserted, "Marivaux n'a fait que répéter, avec mille variantes, détours et subtilités, des situations sentimentales qui sont plus sobrement traitées et avec moins de marivaudage, c'est certain, dans *La Princesse d'Elide*."[6] This statement is particularly important because Marivaux is credited with having written a number of *surprise* plays.[7]

More recent Marivaux specialists have admitted, in part, that Marivaux owes a certain amount of inspiration to Molière. Gustave Larroumet declared: "Avec Marivaux, la comédie entre dans une période nouvelle. Il ne se rattachait directement à aucun de ses devanciers. [Il était] Très désireux de ne pas les imiter, même les plus illustres," and in a footnote Larroumet commented, "Telle était du moins son intention; en réalité il n'a pu se garder complètement de

[3]McKee, *Theater of Marivaux*, 5-6.
[4]Cited by Marcel Arland, *Marivaux* (Paris: Gallimard, 1950), 102-103.
[5]Ferdinand Brunetière, "Marivaux et Molière," *Revue des deux mondes* (1 April 1881):675.
[6]Maurice Donnay, *Molière* (Paris: Arthème Fayard, 1911), 309.
[7]Gustave Larroumet, *Marivaux, sa vie et ses oeuvres* (Paris: Hachette, 1881), 153-154, credits Marivaux with ten *surprise* plays: *Arlequin poli par l'amour, La Surprise de l'amour, La Double inconstance, La (Seconde) Surprise de l'amour, Le Jeu de l'amour et du hasard, Les Serments indiscrets, L'Heureux stratagème, Les Fausses confidences, L'Epreuve*, and *La Dispute*.

réminiscences de détail."[8] Marcel Arland, however, developed the question more explicitly, although in too general a tone and without having recourse to textual examples.

> Qu'il n'ait aimé Molière, c'est possible. . . . Peut-être aussi, à l'antipathie déclarée de Marivaux à l'égard de Molière, faut-il voir la réaction naturelle d'un génie qui veut se préserver d'une redoutable influence. . . . Il lui arrive d'ailleurs de trouver un appui chez son grand aîné, là où coincident leurs natures, par exemple pour certaines querelles d'amoureux, certains traits de moeurs, de caractère, ou telle satire de l'éducation; là aussi où s'imposent, hors de toute nature particulière, les exigences fondamentales de la scène. Au demeurant, il existe entre eux un lien plus profond.[9]

The extent and nature of this *lien* has not been defined yet because "so little scholarship has been devoted to Marivaux's theater that the subject is fraught with unresolved literary problems, such as the exact extent of Molière's influence on Marivaux."[10] And, as a matter of fact, this *lien* still gives birth to what might appear as contradictory statements: for despite the opening sentences of his introduction, and having fully developed his subject, Kenneth N. McKee agrees that "much as Marivaux disliked Molière, he could not entirely escape his influence."[11]

Yet E. J. H. Greene went so far as to call the entire vogue of the *rapprochement* of the two playwrights as nothing but "a red herring, one that should be thrown out."[12] This, in spite of the fact that throughout his book he perceives frequent similarities, not only worth noting but also giving rise to rather detailed, lengthy discussions. Like many Marivaux *aficionados*, the commentator, pleased by the current popular revival of the seventeenth-century playwright, bestows on the latter qualities of extreme inventiveness, which he need not have had in order to explain his successes. If, as one shall see, Marivaux recalled Molière persistently in about one-half of his total theatrical production, and less often in his novels, he did so almost always without falling into the trap of plagiarism: that is, his imitation of Molière adhered to the age-old tradition followed by the best of writers who compose in approximately the same way, and who express approximately the same feelings and preoccupations that a masterful predecessor would have, had he been alive and active at the same time. This is how Corneille and Racine, for example, have imitated the ancients.

That, outside of his recollections of Molière, Marivaux's multifaceted originality appears indisputable is not a point that needs to be

[8]*Ibid.*, 155-156.
[9]Arland, *Marivaux*, 103-104.
[10]McKee, *Theater of Marivaux*, viii.
[11]*Ibid.*, 263.
[12]Greene, *Marivaux*, 222.

belabored long. However, equally beyond question is the fact that the seventeenth-century playwright had bequeathed such a strong tradition of the comedy of *humour* laced with social satire and had depicted so many "types" (the social climber, the hypochondriac, the religious hypocrite, the atheist, the misanthrope, the impertinent, the ambitious, the babbler, and so on) that early eighteenth-century playwrights found the field severely circumscribed. There was, of course, the *commedia dell'arte*, the premises of which were less psychological and less polemical, and on which a writer intent on avoiding being overwhelmed by the *moliéresque* tradition could draw more freely. Moreover, the Italian imports and the French popularization of them had their own set of permanent types: the bigot, the lover, the comic, impudent servant, the authoritarian father, the dotty rival, and others, all embroiled in true-to-life and not so true-to-life adventures interspersed with farcical *lazzi* of assorted zany personages. But the world of the *commedia,* whimsical as it was, and in spite of the fact that it had very few philosophical, moral, or social pretentions of any kind, had appealed also to Molière. The latter's digs against doctors, cuckolded husbands, pedantic women, and other controversial personages, were modeled at least partly on the peppered sketches (it will be recalled that the presentations of the *commedia* were based on sketches, not on written plays) that the Italians had introduced. Therefore, the heritage left by Molière was so all-encompassing that, whether Marivaux chose to compose formal or informal comedies, it was still difficult to steer clear of *moliéresque* detail. Besides, his wish to remain original notwithstanding, full-fledged efforts to ignore entirely the typical *moliéresque* ingredients that had survived would have been, from the point of view of the dramatist who wished success, unwarranted and unwise.

The great difference between Marivaux and Molière appears to reside in the former's ability to express that which the latter had thought of minor importance and preferred to leave in the background. Love, for Molière, was what tottering wooers or grouchy old men talked about. Love was not a serious preoccupation, and hardly ever was it an obsession. Obsessions there were, but with other concerns: money, social climbing, religious devotion, relationship with one's doctors, and so on. A miser ordering a miserly dinner or a doctor's prescription of medicine, for example, provided for scenes that surpassed in importance any love plot or subplot that might otherwise be present. On the contrary, Marivaux relegated peculiarities, follies, and vices to a minor role in order to bring to the fore the lovers themselves. These are sometimes young, and often adults, but their chronological age, like their social status, makes very little difference. For them, love is always an emotion requiring analysis, dissection even. Thus Marivaux's personages engage in a dual role: that of loving and that of watching, as a spectator might, the birth and growth of love. The first part needed to be played still in accordance with prescribed social decorum; after all, in the early eighteenth century, family considerations, as in the century of Molière, limited one's exuberance and paled one's overtness. On the contrary, there is much more freedom in acting out the second part. In fulfilling it, the lover-examiner-of-love watches it emerge unexpectedly, states his or her surprise, hides it at times and causes it to become unmasked at others, alternatively observing it vanish and surge aroused again, piqued, irritated, held back, offered to the wrong person, and finally settled where it belongs. Such subtle analysis of tender moods brings out the infinite variety of little conflicts that pride and vanity, and caprice and misunderstanding may produce before the certainty of love is finally attained. In addition, the personages' sudden realization of what love means, their attempt to struggle against it, to make certain of their feelings, and to assure themselves of the genuineness of another's devotion, to detect the motives and to distinguish between shades of difference, required that Marivaux supply all the verbal quibbles in the battle of wits between his contending men and women. The exchanges needed a special vocabulary within an arsenal of ingenious plays on words and refinements of thought, which gave to his style a flavor all its own. This style, which is a combination of the casuistry of love and witty dialog in delicate, figurative language, is what critics have called *marivaudage*, a quality lacking entirely in the theater of Molière. Whereas Marivaux's minor characters chose, in part, the speech characteristics of his more robust predecessor, most of his other personages opted instead for a certain finesse of language in their efforts to penetrate more deeply the intricate pathways of the heart. It is not quite without reason, therefore, that one commentator made the following unexpected remark: "Molière is roast beef to his [Marivaux's] lemon soufflé."[13]

A more frequent comparison has been made with the painter Watteau, who did many portraits of various actors of the Comédie Italienne. The resemblance between the two artists bears on the scenes and figures presented by them in different media, but each interpreting and supplementing the other. Often Marivaux's themes may be likened to some kind of *Embarquement pour Cythère*, although his groups are not so numerous as in Watteau's paintings. For both, however, the final destination is almost always matrimony, in which state we may assume

---

[13] Mandel, *Seven Comedies by Marivaux*, 9.

that the well-matched pairs will live happily ever after. In fact, the happy ending of Marivaux's comedies contrasts pointedly with the often sad and unsure dénouements of those of Molière. Morever, in the case of the seventeenth-century playwright, the spectator could be distracted from the less felicitous episodes (whether occurring before or at the end of a play) by the buffoonery and slapstick farce that the author had inherited from the *Commedia*. On the contrary, no such distraction was necessary for the viewer or reader of Marivaux's comedies since the playwright could anticipate the happy endings he was going to present. Thus, while his plays are nevertheless lively, the tone remains almost always decent, whether it be expressed in the humor of masters or in that of servants. Delicacy and refinement of language prevail, no easy task when one has to vary the form of expression in order to suit the personage and his station in life. Marivaux excels in this undertaking by utilizing always a different choice of words or turns of phrases to distinguish the master from the valet and the mistress from the soubrette.

The almost total decency and moral tone of his comedies are in sharp contrast with those of Molière and with the manners of the Regency that influenced the followers of Molière in the early eighteenth century. Although Marivaux retains clever servants and numerous intrigues, the latter are far different from the unscrupulous designs and frequently immoral deeds of Molière's Sganarelles, of the Crispins, and the Frontins of Regnard or Lesage, for example. A certain undertone of innocence is maintained, and this, in turn, leads to a reduction of external action in general and of violence in particular. The forces within dominate, and the inner struggles of the personages often are likened to those of the characters of Racine's theater. As in the case of the seventeenth-century tragedy writer, Marivaux's comedies are marked by the supremacy of love, by the author's penetrating psychology of this sentiment, studied, however, in its lighter moods, and by the playwright's predilection for emphasizing feminine parts, which are predominant in most of his plays. Like Racine, also, Marivaux is skillful in maintaining the interest of the spectator with a minimum of plot (plots were often complex in Moliére's theater), and he moves easily within the three unities required by classical decorum. Having fewer characters on the stage and only a short journey to go with them (usually from the birth to the declaration of love), Marivaux is able to stick with his personages minute step by minute step. In this, he breaks not only with Molière but with the entire tradition of the French and Italian comedy, which always bustled with much activity, was mad crisscross with thwarted lovers, and contained a rich gallery of characters moving within a frequently fantastic whirl of events. There was little time in those plays for much control of the half-tone, or for the trembling uncertainty in which Marivaux was interested for the purpose of bringing out psychological detail. Thus, it may be said quite bluntly that the eighteenth-century playwright was the first in Western Europe to reduce a comic action to a Racinian minimum in order to make time for the close inspection of love.

Yet, such inspection must not be understood as signifying the analysis of expressions of passion or of scenes of very intimate tenderness. Marivaux's characters are cool by comparison to those of Molière. A single sentence or a single gesture suffices to confess love, and one never finds the pomposity of an Alceste or a Tartuffe. Love has nothing cynical or ferocious about it. There is only amiability and indulgence, aspects, of course, that the more robust did not appreciate and branded as feminine.[14]

But be that as it may, it is a fact that Marivaux's young ladies are more sprightly, more attractive, and better observed than their suitors. Whereas Molière had depicted his female personages in such a way as to bestow upon them much vigor, at times stubborness, and often qualities that detracted from their femininity, such as immoderation, extreme shrewdness, contrivance, even dishonesty; Marivaux's girls remain feminine. True, we see now and then a coquette who jilts a man, but she quickly longs for him when he neglects her. Of course, Marivaux does write episodes in which a young, flirtatious thing swears fidelity to one man, only to fall in love with another. Yet frivolity does not degenerate into dishonesty; a certain amount of time passes, and, in addition, in her embarrassment she attempts to suppress into the unconscious the emotion that now is addressed to someone else. More often, however, girls simply wait and tremble before a declaration of love is made by or to them. They sigh, weep, affirm, and believe in their sincerity even if readers and spectators do not. And they always maintain a certain amount of innocence and purity, purging them and providing some relief from the recollection of the more quarrelsome and more pugnacious, if more witty, women of Molière.

Marivaux's young men are delineated less well. Their temperament is, in general, devoid of the virility required to distinguish them beyond any doubt from the maidens whom they court. Their lack of toughness makes them blush often, remain timid, swoon, sometime even weep. At any rate, they sigh and implore too ardently; bashfulness makes them blind and deaf to the most obvious advances; and often one feels like kicking them and telling them what should have been obvious a long

---

[14]See earlier discussion, Emile Faguet's remark on Marivaux.

time ago. Yet in spite of the tone *larmoyant* and the *attendrissement* that one notes in their character, they do have redeeming qualities, such as their lack of extreme slyness and the fact that they are never real villains. Unlike the personages of the followers of Molière in the 1720's, Marivaux's young men hardly ever use coarse or indelicate words, and they remain free from any indecorous reference. They would never say, for example, like one of Autreau's young wooers, "Vive l'amant habile et le mari stupide," or refer to a girl as "une poule capricieuse et rusée, à la recherche d'un mari idiot." Nor would Marivaux ever have described a wedding performed by a notary public whose name is Cornelio Cornetto. Although the then famous Deportes could have one of his male characters refer in 1721 to a scarf hiding a girl's breasts, and remark: "Mieux vaut ne pas les avoir . . . que de n'en pas être fière," the young men of Marivaux banished from their speech anything that might have detracted from their more placid but less debatable personality.

It can be said that the playwright's treatment of young lovers led him to internalize the action so that, even though the plays contained a certain amount of trickery, the spectators' awareness nevertheless could focus on the real persons rather than on the artificial pranks. What happens, in effect, is that the author does use, although never pompously and never in anger, representations of spite, vanity, cunning, envy, trickery, snobbery, and the like; but he remains nevertheless equidistant from the brutality of Molière in the preceding century, and that of Lesage and Regnard in his own, as he does from the extreme sentimentality of Nivelle de la Chaussée and Diderot. His young men and women may have shortcomings, but they do not have vices. Morover, their faults are placed side by side with mellow kindliness, amiable tolerance, and human sensibility. There is little place in Marivaux's work for Molière's cynicism. Although Marivaux, like his predecessor, is an Epicurian, that is, willing to allow men, and especially women, the weaknesses from which he knows hardly anyone is exempt, he sheds no tears over lost virtue; he appears simply to suggest forgiveness. Tricks and pranks make life more palatable, he suggests, and one ought never worship Man, nor engage in revelation, commination, or prophecy. Molière kept repeating that he only wanted to please, but he got caught, nevertheless, in the trap of his own profundity: he philosophized and he taught frequently explicit lessons. On the contrary, Marivaux was less ambitious and viewed his art as the high sport of the intellect, which results in decoration, diversion, above all in an unfaltering grace. Not that there are no lessons to be derived from his comedies, or that moralizing is totally absent; there are ideas, as there

are sensuality, satire, wit, and tenderness, but only as far as graceful-
ness allows. His transparence and mobility are unlike those of Molière,
who had used the come-and-go of moods, actions, and decisions
without much concern for grace. Marivaldian realism, however, marries sensibility to Epicurianism, and the result is an equilibrium that
Gustave Larroumet had defined when he spoke of "cette ironie assagie
par la bonté, aimable et caressante même lorsqu'elle se met en colère,
cette douce gaieté . . . cette verve pleine d'ordre et de contrôle, cette
fleur d'élégance et de courtoisie."[15]

Marivaux's verve benefited, of course, from the example set by the
various salons that he frequented. Although Molière had scorned the
salons of his time, being too busy and too independent to see in them
anything other than a target of mockery, Marivaux was one of the
habitués of such celebrated gatherings as those conducted by Madame
de Lambert, Madame de Tencin, and Madame du Deffand. The first,
from 1720 onward, received every Tuesday and Wednesday, Tuesday
being the day for men of letters. Marivaux had occasion to meet in her
salon such famous writers as Fontenelle and La Motte, and a few years
later even Montesquieu. After Madame de Lambert's death in 1733, it
was Madame de Tencin who took over the "Tuesdays," and Fontenelle,
La Motte, and Marivaux were among the very few who were privileged
to have dinner with the hostess before the arrival of the other guests. It
was in her salon that the eighteenth-century playwright was exposed to
the aristocratic *femmes galantes* and *femmes d'esprit* of the time. Under
their influence, conversation in these salons was remarkable for its wit
and grace. Discussion was considered to be a sport of the mind, each
participant being very careful to seize upon the right moment for the
insertion of his own remark, his story or anecdote, often light and
sometimes artificial, yet contributing to the graceful surroundings. It is
known that Madame de Tencin admired greatly Marivaux's contribu-
tions and made consistent efforts in the course of meetings to make
certain that his points of view and the sparkle of his phraseology charm,
as it so often did, the hostess and her guests. In fact, it was her
admiration of him as a nonpompous discussant that prompted her to
engage in untiring efforts to gain for him the necessary votes for election
to the Academy. It was she who managed to win for her friend the
support of the Duke of Richelieu, for example, who otherwise would
have given his vote to Voltaire. Marivaux's belief in *la nécessité d'avoir
toujours de l'esprit* fit the requirements of the eighteenth-century salons. According to D'Alembert, who was also an *habitué* of Madame du
Deffand, the refinement and sagacity of the conversation that Marivaux

[15]Larroumet, *Marivaux, sa vie et ses oeuvres*, 509.

practiced in the course of the meetings were transferred by him to the characters of his plays. This is corroborated by Marivaux himself in the preface to *Les Serments indiscrets*, in which he wrote that he tried to reproduce the general tone he encountered in the salons. It is known also that the playwright's famous account of the dinner party at Madame de Dorsin's, in the course of which he has Marianne emphasize that what counted most was the effortlessness and natural ease with which conversation was carried on, is modeled after Madame de Tencin's own dinner parties, and that the latter furnished the model for Madame de Dorsin. It is no surprise, then, that Marivaux's comedies should differ from those of Molière with respect to the importance of subtlety, sympathetic affability, and grace. Because he was schooled by the salons, where he found a natural complement to his own personality, it was impossible for him not to reproduce their ambiance and manner of expression.

Having said all of the above, it appears, nevertheless, that after Molière, it was very difficult to continue to invent. Marivaux's predecessor had inserted into comedy the image of human nature, with most of its eternal traits, as well as the image of French society, with its particular characteristics. Molière's ability to summarize in several personages the quintessence of numberless models, his exhaustion, over a long period of time, of great comical plots, resulted in a certain limitation that Marivaux, no matter how much he wanted to diminish, was unable to obliterate. If the eighteenth-century playwright succeeded, however, in extending and altering somewhat the *moliéresque* domains, as was pointed out above, his recollections of the famous predecessor go beyond the mere coincidental. In the following chapters, an attempt will be made to show the exact relationship between the two playwrights through comparison of the texts themselves in order to settle, in a more definitive way, the opposing views that Marivaux and Molière specialists have had, to date, on the subject.

LE PERE PRUDENT ET EQUITABLE

According to Kenneth N. McKee, "It should be noted that as a youth Marivaux imitated Molière, although some fifteen years later as a professional playwright in Paris he consistently refused to follow the Molière tradition."[1] Although there are some reservations to be made about the latter part of the statement, the first part of it is true, and it is the purpose of this chapter to determine the extent to which Marivaux, who was only eighteen at the time and living in Limoges, was influenced by Molière in *Le Père prudent et équitable*.

According to an anecdote reported by La Porte in 1759, Marivaux's first comedy, a one-act piece in verse, was written in only one week for the purpose of winning a bet that challenged his powers of inventiveness. A quick look at the commonplace plot, which supports very little the title, and is, moreover, written in often faulty versification, corroborates La Porte's story. The father, Démocrite, decides to marry his daughter, Philine, to one of three proposed pretenders: Ariste, a rather aged farmer, the more subtle Chevalier de la Minardinière, or the selfish Financier. Philine, however, loves Cléandre, a young man not too intelligent, but poor enough to win her sympathy. As often happens in the plays of the period, the lovers have a spat about an insignificant subject, whereupon Crispin, the valet of Cléandre, takes matters into his own hands and, in order to prevent the marriage of Philine to any of the other three suitors, intercepts each and, through appropriate theatrical antics, tries to turn them away from the proposed marriage. In order to dissuade Ariste, he has Toinette, Philine's maid, pose as Démocrite's daughter. She engages in such brazen effrontery in her talk with and attitude toward Ariste that any man would have to be a fool to marry her no matter how much he might be in love. To inspire Philine's disgust for the Chevalier de la Minardinière in front of the latter's rival, Crispin dresses as a woman in order to tell the family that she is the abandoned mistress of the irresponsible pretender, who allegedly leads a very fast and notorious existence. And when the Financier appears, Crispin informs him quite bluntly that Philine has some unspeakable and incurable disease, some relic of her *past*, which would make marriage morally wrong and physically dangerous. Faced with these revelations, the father, who might be *équitable* but is certainly not *prudent*, has no recourse but to yield to his daughter's love for Cléandre. This he does with ease since, as a *deus ex machina* would have it, Cléandre becomes rich overnight, having won some unexpected lawsuit. The three suitors then disappear, the marriage of

---

[1]McKee, *Theater of Marivaux*, 15.

Philine to her *amant* will take place, and they reportedly will live happily ever after.

Even a cursory perusal of the story indicates that almost everything in it is derivative. A father's insistence that his daughter marry someone she does not love, the lovers' quarrel, the interference and help of servants, the parent's final abandonment of his plans, and the satisfactory solution of the problem finally brought about by an outside intervention are all commonplaces in the dramatic literature of the period. Marivaux's concern with winning a bet and winning it within a few days' time, explains in part the lack of originality of *Le Père prudent et équitable*. His willingness to borrow excessively for his first theatrical undertaking, however, does not diminish from the importance of the play, which is one of those significant first productions of a young man embarking on a literary career that is going to comprise certain preferences for dramatic devices common to most comedies: disguises, *quiproquos*, spicy language on the part of servants, imprudent elders, and rather silly lovers. Paul Gazagne and Frédéric Deloffre,[2] while pointing to the lack of originality of *Le Père prudent et équitable*, fail, nevertheless, to specify exactly the origin of the material that the author might have used. On the contrary, Gustave Larroumet notes, but without giving specific textual examples, that the play "est une comédie d'écolier, toute d'imitation, pleine de reminiscences de . . . Molière."[3] In fact, when an attempt at specificity is made by the critic who later points to the similarities between *Le Père prudent et équitable* and Molière's *Monsieur de Pourceaugnac*, he commits an error: he compares Scene 15 of Marivaux's play with Act III, Scene 1 of Molière's comedy, the latter scene allegedly taking place between Sbrigani and Monsieur de Pourceaugnac; Act III, Scene 1 of Molière's play, however, takes place between Julie, Eraste, and Narine. Moreover, there is no connection between Scene 15 of Marivaux's comedy and III, 1, of Molière's. There may be a question as to the edition of Molière used by Gustave Larroumet and the arrangement of scenes in that edition. Larroumet, however, does not reveal the edition he used. Kenneth N. McKee is more precise when he states that "the lovers' quarrel in Scene 3 is reminiscent of the quarrel between Marianne and Valère in *Le Tartuffe*,"[4] but he does not compare the dialogue in question.

---

[2]*Cf*. Paul Gazagne, *Marivaux par lui-même* (Paris: Editions du Seuil, 1954), 6; and Frédéric Deloffre, *Marivaux et le marivaudage: Etude de langue et de style* (Paris: Les Belles Lettres, 1955), 81-85.

[3]Larroumet, *Marivaux, sa vie et ses oeuvres*, 15.

[4]McKee, *Theater of Marivaux*, 155.

There is little doubt that *Le Tartuffe* served as a model for Marivaux's play. To begin with, the situations are alike: in both comedies, a father refuses to marry his daughter to the man of her choice, and instead attempts to select another or others for her; in both, the girl oscillates between love and duty, and in both, the rejected male lover is prone to more drastic measures than the girl is courageous enough to follow; finally, in both comedies, the two lovers quarrel and a servant attempts to terminate the argument by effecting a reconciliation and a plan that will frustrate the father and please the lovers. It may be stipulated, of course, that there is much in the structure outlined above that is common to the theater of the time. Marivaux might have borrowed from anybody, or he might have composed naturally, as his contemporaries did, simply because writers often are carried along by the themes current in their time. Nevertheless, the lovers' quarrel interrupted by the servant's attempts to terminate it is not too common in early eighteenth-century dramatic literature. This is a theme characteristic of Molière, and the verbal similarities between the scenes in question leave little doubt as to the source of influence on Marivaux.

Scene 3 of Act II of *Le Tartuffe*, in which Dorine tries to frighten Marianne by describing to her the life she would lead in her future husband's small town "en oncles et en cousins fertile," where, she says, "dans le carnaval, vous pourrez espérer le bal et la grande bande," but, she adds, "à savoir, deux musettes" only, appears to have served as a model for Crispin's not so subtle warnings in Scene 12:

Oui, oui, parmi les vaches, les dindons,
Il vous fera beau voir de rubans tout ornée!
Dans huit jours vous serez couleur de cheminée.
Tous ses biens sont ruraux, il faut beaucoup de soins.

In Molière's play, upon learning of the father's decision, Valère asks of Marianne, "Et quel est le dessein où votre âme s'arrête, Madame?" and Marianne replies, "Je ne sais" (II, 4). In Marivaux's comedy, the same situation gives birth to a similarly constructed piece of dialogue:

CLEANDRE: A quoi vous déterminez-vous?

PHILINE: A rien. (Scene 3)

In the quarrel that ensues, both pairs of rejected lovers share the same sentiments and word their plans for the future in a similar manner.

MARIANNE: Vous vous consolerez assez facilement.
VALERE: J'y ferai mon possible, et vous le pouvez croire
    Un coeur qui nous oublie engage notre gloire;
    Il faut à l'oublier mettre aussi tous nos soins;
    Et cette lâcheté jamais ne se pardonne,
    De montrer de l'amour pour qui nous abandonne. (II, 4)

Compare now Cléandre's words to those of Valère above.

> N'attendez pas de moi de marques de douleur;
> On ne perd presque rien à perdre un mauvais coeur;
> Et ce serait montrer une faiblesse extrême,
> Par de lâches transports de prouver qu'on vous aime. (Scene 3)

Note especially the similarity between the noun *lâcheté* used by Valère, and the modified noun *lâches transports* employed by Cléandre. A further resemblance exists between the stage indications given by the two authors. Molière directs Valère as follows: *"Il fait un pas pour s'en aller . . . revenant encore . . . en sortant . . . revenant encore . . . s'en va, et, lorsqu'il est vers la porte, il se retourne"* (II, 4). Marivaux, whose dramatic action resides more in the heart of his personages, nevertheless directs the actor playing Cléandre in much the same way: *"Il s'en va et il revient"* (Scene 3).

Moreover, Dorine's attempts to effect a reconciliation between Valère and Marianne in Molière's play may be compared to Toinette's efforts in Marivaux's. Dorine commands:

> Cessez ce badinage; et venez ça tous deux . . .
> Vous bien remettre ensemble et vous tirer d'affaire . . .
> Etes-vous fous d'avoir un pareil démêlé . . .
> Pour une autre saison laissons tout ce débat,
> Et songeons à parer ce fâcheux mariage. (II, 4)

And Toinette orders:

> Finissez vos débats, et calmez le chagrin . . .
> Que vous êtes enfants . . .
> Eh bien! finissez-vous . . .
> Mais, Madame, en un mot, cessez ce badinage. (Scene 3)

Thus, the last words of Toinette correspond exactly to the first few words of Dorine: *Cessez ce badinage*.

After reviewing the resemblances pointed out above, one may conclude that Scene 3 of *Le Père prudent et équitable* is built according to the model furnished by the lovers' quarrel in *Le Tartuffe*, and that Marivaux is here (as is often the case with a young and inexperienced author) at the border of plagiarism. Later in his career, the influence of Molière will be less apparent, most often in an inverse proportion to the maturity and experience the playwright will attain.

Le Père prudent et équitable, however, shows not only the recollection of *Le Tartuffe*, but even to a greater extent that of *Monsieur de Pourceaugnac*. Scene 15 of Marivaux's play follows closely Act II, Scene 2 of Molière's. In Molière's comedy, Monsieur de Pourceaugnac arrives for the purpose of contracting a marriage with Julie, who, naturally, is in love with someone else. Eraste, the man she loves, has two doctors inform the girl's father that Monsieur de Pourceaugnac has some kind of venereal disease.

PREMIER MEDECIN: Vous avez, monsieur, un certain monsieur de Pourceaugnac
    qui doit épouser votre fille?
ORONTE:Oui, je l'attends de Limoges, et il devrait être arrivé.

PREMIER MEDECIN: Aussi l'est-il, et il s'en est fui, de chez moi, après y avoir été
    mis; mais je vous défends, de la part de la médecine, de procéder au
    mariage que vous avez conclu, que je ne l'aie dûment préparé pour cela, et
    mis en état de procréer des enfants bien conditionnés de corps et d'esprit.

ORONTE: Comment donc?

PREMIERMEDECIN: Votre prétendu gendre a été constitué mon malade; sa
    maladie, qu'on m'a donnée à guérir . . .

ORONTE: Il a quelque mal?

PREMIER MEDECIN: Oui.

ORONTE: Et quel mal, s'il vous plaît?

PREMIER MEDECIN: Ne vous en mettez pas en peine.

ORONTE: Est-ce quelque mal . . .

PREMIER MEDECIN: Les médecins sont obligés au secret. (II, 2)

In much the same manner, Crispin, former servant of the Financier who now works for Cléandre, attempts to turn his former master away from the projected marriage with Philine by insinuating that she has an incurable disease.

CRISPIN: Quoi! vous vous alleiz avec cette famille!

LE FINANCIER: Eh! ne fais-je pas bien?

CRISPIN: Je suis de la maison et je ne puis parler.

LE FINANCIER: Tu me donnes soupçon . . .

CRISPIN: Je n'ose vous rien dire.

LE FINANCIER: Quoi! tu me cacherais . . .

CRISPIN: Je n'aime point à nuire.

LE FINANCIER: Crispin, encore un coup . . . parle donc.

CRISPIN: Eh bien donc! cette fille,
    Son père et ses parents et toute la famille,
    Tombent d'un certain mal que je n'ose nommer. (Scene 15)

A further similarity exists between Act II, Scene 8 of Molière's play and Scene 21 of Marivaux's. As an additional obstacle in the path of marriage between Monsieur de Pourceaugnac and Julie, Molière has Lucette, *femme d'intrigue*, pretend in front of Oronte that she is Monsieur de Pourceaugnac's wife.

LUCETTE, *contrefaisant une languedocienne:* Ah! tu es assi, et a la fi yeu te trobi après abé fait tant de passés. Podes-tu, scélérat, podes-tu soustent ma bisto?

MONSIEUR DE POURCEAUGNAC: Qu'est-ce que veut cette femme-là?

LUCETTE: Que te boit, infâme! Tu fas semblan de nou me pas connouisse, et nou rougisses pas, impudint que tu sois, tu ne rougisses pas de me beyre? *(A Oronte)* Nou sabi pas, moussur, saquos bos dont m'an dit que bouillo espousa la fillo; may yeu bous déclari que yeu soun sa fenno, et que y a set ans, moussur, qu'en passan à Pézénas, el auguet l'adresse, dambé sas mignardisos, como sap tapla fayre, de me gaigna lou cor, et m'oubligel pra quel mayen a ly douna la man per l'espousa.

ORONTE: Oh! oh!

LUCETTE: Lou traite me quittel tres ans après . . . may dins lou tens qui soungeabi lou mens, m'en dounat abist, que begnio dins aquesto bilo, per se remarida dambé un autro jouena fillo, que sous parens ly an prooucurado, sensse saupré res de son prumie mariatge . . .

ORONTE: Je ne saurais m'empêcher de pleurer. *(A Monsieur de Pourceaugnac)* Allez, vous êtes un méchant homme. (II, 8)

Likewise, in Marivaux's play, Crispin, dressed as a woman, pretends to be the abandoned wife of the Chevalier de la Minardinière.

CRISPIN, *déguisé en femme:* N'est-ce pas vous, Monsieur, qu'on nomme Démocrite?

DEMOCRITE: Oui . . .

CRISPIN: Mais enfin, il est temps d'avouer mon malheur . . .
J'aime depuis longtemps un chevalier parjure,
Qui sut de ses serments déguiser l'imposture.
Le cruel! J'eus pitié de tous ses feints tourments;
Hélas! de son bonheur je hâtai les moments.
Je l'épousai, Monsieur: mais notre mariage,
A l'insu des parents, se fit dans un village;
Et, croyant avoir mis ma conscience en repos,
Je me livrai, Monsieur, pour comble de tous maux.
Il différa toujours de m'avouer pour femme . . .
Cet ingrat chevalier épouse votre fille!

DEMOCRITE: Quoi! c'est lui qui veut entrer dans ma famille?

CRISPIN: Lui-même! vous voyez la noire trahison.

DEMOCRITE: Cette action est noire. (Scene 21)

Although it is true that servants who disguise themselves to outwit elders and aid a young master are prolific in the plays of the time (see *Le Légataire universel* of Regnard, *La Folle enchère* of Dancourt, and the like), here the details are strikingly similar: Monsieur de Pourceaugnac convinces Lucette to marry him *dambé sas mignardisos,* and the Chevalier won Crispin by means of *feints tourments;* Monsieur de Pourceaugnac's parents do not know of their son's marriage, and the marriage of the Chevalier likewise is performed *à l'insu des parents;* finally, both alleged husbands abandon their wives and are about to commit bigamy. However, the comic effect of Molière's use of the language of a *languedocienne* is lacking in Marivaux's episode.

It should be noted also that, if borrowing from Molière appears rather extended in *Le Père prudent et équitable,* the influence of Regnard is not to be neglected, because likewise it played a role in Marivaux's composition. In Regnard's play, there is also a Crispin who assumes the role of a nephew from Normandy and a niece from Maine in order to cause doubt in the mind of Géronte. But not only is the situation generally the same, some of the words used by Marivaux's Crispin appear to have been taken from those of the personage of Regnard. Marivaux's lines: "Remue, un peu, Crispin, ton imaginative . . . Dieu, quel enthousiasme . . . le dessein que j'enfante," *etc.,* from Scene 3, are an echo of Regnard's lines: "J'accouche d'un dessein . . . exerce à ce sujet ton imaginative . . . Ne troublez pas l'enthousiasme où je suis," of the second scene of Act II of *Le Légataire.* Another line, "Je te fonde, Crispin, une sûre cuisine," in Scene 4 of Marivaux's comedy, may have its in origin in "C'est sur mon bien seul qu'il fonde sa cuisine" of Act III, Scene 3 of Regnard's play.

Regnard's influence, however, is minor by comparison to that of Molière. Marivaux's reliance on certain episodes in *Le Tartuffe* and in *Monsieur de Pourceaugnac* is specific enough and extended enough to make one conclude that he turned to his predecessor rather un-abashedly for his first dramatic endeavor. *Aficionados* of Marivaux, who usually try to belittle the *moliéresque* influence, almost invariably point to the fact that many so-called *moliéresque* themes are not original with Molière. By implication, they advance the opinion that Marivaux might have borrowed from anybody or simply might have written in accordance with unattributable literary recollections, which he used only subconsciously. One may agree readily with Henry Carrington Lancaster, who points out, for example, that the theme of the pretended malady is not original with Molière, and that it is used in a sixteenth-century play entitled *Les Contens,* by Odet de Turnèbe, in which Geneviève is falsely accused by Françoise of having *un chancre au tétin* (I, 8).[5] But it is difficult to conceive of an eighteen-year-old playwright going back to an almost entirely forgotten sixteenth-century composi-tion for inspiration when the very popular *Monsieur de Pourceaugnac* was, in fact, so much more at hand. On the contrary, in view of the presence of other *moliéresque* episodes and vocabulary in *Le Père*

---

[5]H. C. Lancaster, *French Dramatic Literature in the Seventeenth Century* (Baltimore: John Hopkins, 1936), 2, 719.

prudent et équitable, the conclusion of Kenneth N. McKee cited at the beginning of this chapter appears correct indeed. The best in Marivaux's play, the lovers' quarrel and certain antics of Crispin, was furnished by Molière, and instead of attempting to ignore the influence of the seventeenth-century dramatist, one ought to compliment Marivaux, who, in a first effort, was smart enough to rely on a brilliant predecessor.

ARLEQUIN POLI PAR L'AMOUR

Neither is Marivaux's second play (and his first successful entry into the French dramatic repertory), as I shall attempt to show, free from a certain number of thematic influences derived from Molière.

It should be pointed out immediately, however, that *Arlequin poli par l'amour* is, nevertheless, the product of an entirely different Marivaux. Now the author is no longer an apprentice. He is an accomplished dramatist who, having undergone the influence of the salons of his time, decides to embark upon the analysis of the birth of love. This he does adroitly by marrying the *lazzi* of the *commedia* with certain typically *moliéresque* antics that he probably borrowed from *Le Bourgeois gentilhomme*. To be sure, there is only a minor connection between the structure of the plot in *Arlequin poli par l'amour* and Molière's play. Marivaux's topic concerns Arlequin, whom The Fairy loves and kidnaps even though she is supposed to marry someone else. In her palace, Arlequin is subjected to The Fairy's attentions, which include a number of lessons designed to make him *poli* (much as the lessons to which Monsieur Jourdain subjects himself are designed to make him a gentleman) and suitable for marriage to her. However, Arlequin becomes interested in the shepherdess Silvia, who is equally unresponsive to the shepherd to whom she previously had given her word. The budding love between Arlequin and Silvia is evoked beautifully by Marivaux, until he has The Fairy's magic at one point paralyze Silvia. In the end, Arlequin manages to neutralize his kidnaper's power by pretending to make love to her and, in so doing, taking from her the magic wand that she had used. Powerless, there is nothing left for her to do but to assent to the inevitable marriage between Arlequin and the shepherdess.

Marivaux's main originality in *Arlequin poli par l'amour* resides in the fact that, for the first time, the type for which his personage stands has been endowed with the capacity to fall in love, whereas before, he had been merely an able performer of burlesque tricks. J. F. La Harpe, who for the most part is critical of Marivaux, praises the dramatist's transformation of the *commedia*'s stock character into "ce personnage idéal qui jusque-là n'avait su que faire rire, et que pour la première fois il rendit intéressant en le rendant amoureux."[1]

In fact, the depiction of the traits of adolescent love was not only a preoccupation of the salons, but it extended also into some of the plays that preceded *Arlequin poli par l'amour*, notably in Autreau's *Les*

---

[1] J. F. La Harpe, *Lycée, ou cours de littérature ancienne et moderne* (Paris: Hachette, 1801), 12, 548.

Amans ignorans, which had been performed in 1720. Xavier de Courville mentioned Autreau's personage as a precursor of that of
Marivaux,[2] but he made no textual comparisons, and I found none so
specific as to merit attention. Frédéric Deloffre suggested another
nebulous source in Cervantes' *Pérsiles y Sigismunda*.[3] It is probable
that, as Kenneth N. McKee argued,[4] Molière's *L'Ecole des femmes* had
served Marivaux more directly, for in it the seventeenth-century playwright had depicted the unforgettable and classic genesis of young love
in Agnès, who shares with Arlequin the same general naiveté and
innocence. But beyond the guileless charm of the two characters, a
close perusal of the two texts reveals no specific similarities worth
mentioning.

On the contrary, Kenneth N. McKee, in noticing Marivaux's stage
indications for the actor playing the role of Arlequin, remarked,
"Shades of M. Jourdain!"[5] although he made no attempt to point to exact
similarities. In fact, the rapport between the two plays is one of tone
more than of vocabulary, thematic rather than particular. It will be
recalled that in Molière's comedy, Monsieur Jourdain strives to forget
the fact that his father had been a simple merchant by acquiring not
only a dancing teacher but also one for music, a fencing master, and a
professor of philosophy. Unlike Arlequin, who would rather eat and
sleep than learn anything, Monsieur Jourdain wants to learn
everything, and he is willing to spend generously for his lessons. Much
of his clumsiness in relation to his teachers, however, may be compared
to Arlequin's reactions to The Fairy's attempts at didactics. In the very
first scene of Molière's play, it becomes apparent that Monsieur Jourdain is not going to master his lessons easily. The dancing teacher
declares at one point, "Je voudrais, pour lui, qu'il se donnât mieux qu'il
ne fait aux choses que nous lui donnons" (I, 1). The apprehension of the
dancing teacher is realized soon when Monsieur Jourdain, who has
practiced at length the art of bowing in order to greet Dorimène,
engages with the latter in the following dialogue.

> MONSIEUR JOURDAIN: *(après avoir fait deux révérences, se trouvant trop près de
> Dorimène):* Un peu plus loin, madame.
>
> DORIMENE: Comment?
>
> MONSIEUR JOURDAIN: Un pas, s'il vous plaît.
>
> DORIMENE: Quoi donc?
>
> MONSIEUR JOURDAIN: Reculez un peu, pour la troisième. (III, 19)

---

[2]Xavier de Courville, *Luigi Riccoboni dit Lélio* (Paris: Droz, 1943), 2, 201.
[3]Frédéric Deloffre, *Mélanges d'histoire littéraire offerts à M. Paul Dimoff* (Paris: Annales
Universitatis Saraviensis, Philosophie-Lettres, 1954), 3, 216.
[4]McKee, *Theater of Marivaux*, 22.
[5]*Ibid.*, 20.

Similarly, although the situation is somewhat different, at the beginning of Marivaux's play when Arlequin seizes The Fairy's ring (which she had only too graciously offered), his kidnaper scolds him in terms that are not unlike many of those used by Monsieur Jourdain's teachers. She advises, "Mon cher Arlequin, un beau garçon comme vous, quand une dame lui présente quelque chose, doit lui baiser la main en le recevant" (Scene 2). Upon hearing this, *"Arlequin alors prend goulûment la main de la fée qu'il baise"* (Scene 2). It is interesting to note, also, that Arlequin's own dancing teacher attempts to show him how to execute properly a bow, and that Marivaux directs the actor in essentially the same way as did Molière; *"Arlequin égaie cette scène de tout ce que son génie peut lui fournir de propre au sujet"* (Scene 2).

It is safe to assume, then, that Marivaux was familiar with Monsieur Jourdain's antics in *Le Bourgeois gentilhomme,* and that the clumsiness of Molière's personage, at least in so far as attempts to execute a bow are concerned, inspired the *lazzi* of Marivaux's character. Such an assumption is corroborated by the fact that both authors saw the comic possibilities of the scene, and, in order to be sure that they are extracted, both directed specifically the play of the actors. An episode involving a social climber who takes dancing lessons had been part of the topic of a previous play, *Fidalgo Aprendiz* by the Portugese author Manuel Melo, almost entirely unknown in Marivaux's time, but of whom Molière might have heard. Marivaux, however, did not know Portugese, and there is no indication that he was at all familiar with the play in question. There is little doubt, however, that the theme of *Le Bourgeois gentilhomme* was part of the common dramatic fund of the time, and in view of the similarities pointed out, Marivaux need not have gone further than Molière for inspiration.

Several other comparisons of minor importance may be made between *Arlequin poli par l'amour* and *Le Bourgeois gentilhomme.* For example, in Molière's comedy when the music teacher has a song performed for his student, the latter's reaction is one of boredom, which he attempts to banish through one of his own interpretations of a more popular and more sensual piece. Likewise, in Marivaux's play, when Arlequin is forced to listen to music and then is asked what he felt during the performance, he responds with different words but with an equally disarming innocence, "Je sens un grand appétit" (Scene 3). And, following further in the footsteps of his predecessor, he reacts to the performance of a ballet by falling asleep, a reaction that Monsieur Jourdain had adopted also when faced with shows that went beyond his powers of comprehension. The one main difference, however, between Monsieur Jourdain and Arlequin is that the former does not profit from his lessons, does not become *poli,* and in fact remains the dupe of his entourage; whereas the latter, at the end of Marivaux's comedy, displays an unexpected ability to outtrick The Fairy, thereby disproving his shaky beginnings in matters of relations between the sexes. Yet, it is this very *originality* on the part of the eighteenth-century playwright that has been considered unacceptable,[6] because it lacks plausibility: one wonders how a young peasant boy can acquire, by means of lessons and by falling in love, more shrewdness and savoir-faire than a Parisian bourgeois in not too dissimilar circumstances. Although there is a fairy and there is magic in the play, it surely was not Marivaux's intention to limit himself to the development of a children's plot. The pastoral and fairyland goings-on in *Arlequin poli par l'amour* notwithstanding, the play combines charm with truth of observation, and this fusion propels it above the level of a light comedy devoid of profound interest.

The charm of *Arlequin poli par l'amour* emerges from the depiction of love as some pilgrimage towards an unknown Cythera, "towards a land transfigured by a light that never was on land or on sea."[7] The truth of Marivaux's observations can be seen in the fact that, in spite of the deceptively simple plot, he engages in a thorough analysis of the actions and reactions of the two main characters, Arlequin and The Fairy. "C'est la pure nature" (Scene 1), comments Trivelin, referring to The Fairy's sudden feelings for Arlequin, and to her capacity to forget instantaneously her previous lover, Merlin. The *naturel* is part of the very fabric of Arlequin and The Fairy. If the former manages to emerge victorious and the latter is defeated, it is because Arlequin, peasant though he is, follows faithfully the dictates of his feelings even though he is not able to recognize them; whereas The Fairy, sophisticated though she is, although identifying the natural spontaneity of her own sentiments and justifying them by placing them above the whimsical and the capricious, is unable to recognize that others are equally deserving of such justification. She is utterly unable to understand that a man could prefer Silvia to her, and labels that as unnatural. Marivaldian genius is, then, perfectly capable of suggesting, within the confines of a pastoral and fairyland plot, psychological verities that are almost scientific in nature: we explain and excuse in ourselves that which we consider unacceptable and reproachable in others. Such qualities, however, require a certain amount of critical effort, which the average spectator surely cannot generate. From a dramatic point of view, then, *Le Bourgeois gentilhomme,* which points to a different but equally true conclusion, namely that one grows old without necessarily

[6]See, for example, the criticism of Jean Fleury, *Marivaux et le marivaudage* (Paris: Plon, 1881), 68.

[7]Arthur Tilley, *Three French Dramatists: Racine, Marivaux, Musset* (New York: Russell and Russell, 1967), 87.

learning anything,[8] is understood more immediately by the mass of spectators who need make less effort in order to understand. Monsieur Jourdain, tricked and deceived until the very end, fulfills better the demands of comicality of Molière's play and satisfies more easily its viewers than does an Arlequin reborn with unexpected flair and discernment in the comedy of Marivaux, whose audience has reason to be surprised, if not startled. "Shades of M. Jourdain" though the eighteenth-century dramatist evoked, his *Arlequin poli par l'amour* lacks the impact of Molière's play. Marivaux's originality, subtle and cerebral, turned against him, as it were, and diminished the potential popularity of his comedy, one that he might have attained had he followed more closely his illustrious predecessor. It is interesting to note that, when the Comédie Française performed *Arlequin poli par l'amour* in November 1955 during one of its tours in America, Walter Kerr, normally suspicious of cerebral imports, wrote: "A lightweight deft powder-box conceit from the featherweight pen of Marivaux had been given such an animated gaiety that it spells out its own simple story with a kick of the heels and an irrepressible bounce into space. . . . Everyone who has strayed into his laquered wonderland is filled with a simple conviction that wonderlands exist." And, recalling the performance of *Le Bourgeois gentilhomme* in the course of the previous week, Kerr added, "The Comédie seems even happier with Marivaux than with its giant, Molière."[9]

It is, of course, difficult to accept the critic's last assertion, for the Comédie presents many more times *Le Bourgeois gentilhomme* than it does *Arlequin poli par l'amour*. On the other hand, the generally favorable opinion that greeted Marivaux's comedy may be explained by the fact that, in this country, we are taken in more easily by wonderlands and we fail to notice the more profound points that a dramatist attempts to suggest, especially when he does so in cryptic fashion. No American reviewer of Marivaux's comedy mentioned The Fairy's justification of the *naturel* in her, nor her refusal to justify the *naturel* in Arlequin. They opted totally, instead, for the fairyland plot, and this may explain Walter Kerr's conclusion.

---

[8]Much as the plays of Samuel Beckett suggest in the twentieth century: see, for example, *La Dernière bande*.

[9]Walter Kerr, *New York Herald Tribune*, 9 November 1955, p. 26.

LA SURPRISE DE L'AMOUR

The title *La Surprise de l'amour* indicates, of course, the type of comedy most closely associated with the author's name. The initial bewilderment caused by the birth of love in the lovers is a theme so marivaldian that the relationship between *La Surprise de l'amour* and at least three of Molière's plays *(Le Dépit amoureux, La Princesse d'Elide, and Le Bourgeois gentilhomme* — more about these associations later) appears astonishing. It is astonishing on a superficial level only, for Marivaux was still in the initial stages of his career in 1722 when his comedy was first presented at the Théâtre Italien, and his earlier exploitations of *moliéresque* topics persuaded him, perhaps, that it was not unwise to continue to complement his own creativity with that of his unequalled predecessor.

There is not much of a plot supporting the psychological dissection of love in *La Surprise de l'amour*. Dramatic interest results more from the analysis of the thoughts and feelings of the characters than from their actions. Lélio and the Countess, unlike lovers in most other plays up to that time, are not in conflict with parents, or guardians, or rivals, or social conventions, or other exterior obstacles; rather they must fight against themselves, that is, against their prejudices, shyness, subdued or declared passions, and other features of the very fabric of their temperaments. Lélio, a Parisian, has been deceived by his mistress and has retired to the country after having vowed to renounce all women. His servant, Arlequin, equally disillusioned, attempts to mirror his master's sentiments, and the two engage in comical, yet serious descriptions of that which is attractive and repelling in the female sex. Both find it impossible to determine the delicate balance between a woman's charm and deceptiveness, yet both suspect that regardless of what this balance might be, man is ultimately helpless to resist. Thus, Marivaux has his characters (as well he ought to in order to stick to psychological truth), engage in tirades the intention of which is to be inimical to women, but whose tone and vocabulary betray the speaker's devotion and capitulation vis-à-vis the fair sex. There are numerous examples in *La Surprise de l'amour* of such marivaldian originality, but one should suffice in this context. "Eh, mon cher enfant, la vipère n'ôte que la vie. Femmes, vous nous ravissez notre raison, notre liberté, notre repos, et vous nous laissez vivre! . . . Quel aimable désordre d'idées dans la tête! L'homme a le bon sens en partage; mais, ma foi, l'esprit n'appartient qu'à la femme . . . . Une femme ne veut être ni tendre, ni dèlicate, ni fâchée, ni bien aise; elle est tout cela sans le savoir, et cela est charmant" (I, 2).

26

The Countess, who is a widow, is just as disdainful of men as Lélio is of women. Her desire to stay away from Lélio parallels his own wish for solitude. Yet circumspect precautions on both sides notwithstanding, Lélio and the Countess meet, write to each other, and otherwise give in to every possible pretext that furthers the commerce between them. Their extreme views regarding the other's sex diminish after each encounter, for theoretical abstractions, after all, do not stand up against flesh and blood, against the surprise of nascent love. Paul Gazagne even went so far as to suggest that, because marriage is not mentioned at the end of the play, the characters' problem is simply one of deciding to sleep together.[1] This is true as far as it goes, but the absolutism of youth that prevails in Lélio and the Countess requires a more permanent solution, marriage perhaps, transcending that suggested by mere physical attraction. The skirmishes that preceed such a solution provide for the comedy of the play, but they also confirm and consolidate the stable emotional security at which the characters arrive before the final curtain. Once concern with self yields to such mutual security, there is no need to specify (such specificity would indeed detract from the dramatic interest awakened) that the future might hold marriage for the Lélio-Countess couple.

It is apparent, then, that the theme of *La Surprise de l'amour* revolves around the usual *dépit* men and women take pleasure in exhibiting. Although *dépit*, in one form or another, was often at the core of comical dramatic situations at the time, similarities between *La Surprise de l'amour* and *moliéresque* themes in several of the comedies by the seventeenth-century playwright have been mentioned by a number of critics, Xavier de Courville, for example wrote:

> Il y a dans Molière un théâtre amoureux, auquel à la vérité il ne s'est pas attardé, mais qui se dessine par example dans . . . *Le Dépit amoureux* et *La Princesse d'Elide*. Le malentendu, si cher à Molière, de deux amants qui se heurtent, se fuient, et se retrouvent, au lieu d'être un délassement grâcieux dans les éclats de la grande comédie, s'étendra, chez Marivaux, à un acte, à trois actes, à cinq actes. La situation de la misanthrope qui se voit forcée d'aimer celui qui fait mine de ne l'aimer pas, au lieu d'être le lien des intermèdes d'une comédie-ballet, deviendra le noeud du drame. Le théâtre de Marivaux est en germe dans celui de Molière: et la première surprise de l'amour c'est *La Princesse d'Elide*.[2]

On the contrary, E. J. H. Greene stated, yet without specifying any reasons, that "in any case it is certainly an error to seek the inspiration of this play in *La Princesse d'Elide*."[3] Although there may be some exaggeration in Xavier de Courville's statement, the specific

---

[1]Gazagne, *Marivaux par lui-même*, 94-95.
[2]Xavier de Courville, *Le Théâtre de Marivaux* (Paris: La Cité des livres, 1930), 1, 65-66.
[3]Greene, *Marivaux*, 57.

similarities that emerge from a comparison of the texts indicate that E. J. H. Greene is not entirely correct either. The exaggeration in the first quotation stems from the critic's playing down of the fact that Marivaux does more than enlarge upon the *malentendu* that he may have borrowed from Molière: the lovers' quarrelsome pirouettes and the final reconciliation are analyzed psychologically by the eighteenth-century playwright, who thus gives to the theme a new dimension absent in Molière. In addition, there appears to be a kind of valueless truism in Courville's sentence, *Le théâtre de Marivaux est en germe dans celui de Molière;* it would not be, perhaps, impossible to prove that anybody's theater is, in germ, in the theater of some predecessor. To illustrate the point in this context, one could go beyond Molière and find strikingly similar instances of amorous spite in other dramatic literature. H. C. Lancaster, for example, showed effectively that "the chief source [for Molière's *Le Dépit amoureux*] is an Italian comedy, Nicolo Secchi's *Interesse* published in 1581."[4] And the same critic proved, in so far as *La Princesse d'Elide* is concerned, that Molière "selected as a model Moreto's *El Desdén con el desdén*."[5] Moreover, immediately after his statement, Xavier de Courville himself noted that in the eighteenth century "Le thème des dédains réciproques avait-il déjà paru sur la scène de la rue Mauconseil: *Rebut pour rebut* en juin 1717, présentait en canevas la pièce de Moreto; en juillet 1718, *Les Amours à la chasse*, de Coypel, rappelaient sur la scène les sonneries de *La Princesse d'Elide*."[6] On the other hand, close perusal of *Rebut pour rebut* and *Les Amours à la chasse* reveals no specific similarities of dialogue, only some of tone and situation. Kenneth N. McKee, who mentions Courville's theory concerning the influence of Molière on Marivaux, makes the point that "the real difference is in the treatment. Certainly there is no connection between the robust farce and not very finely etched spite in *La Princesse d'Elide* and the delicate gradations of love expressed in *La Surprise de l'amour*. To interpret Molière as Marivaux's model strikes a false note. In terms of style and conception Marivaux owes nothing to Molière."[7] Whereas delicacy is not a term with which one usually describes any play of Molière, and whereas gradations of love are indeed present in most of Marivaux's comedies, as will be shown below, Marivaux's acquaintance with the theater of his predecessor was such that very definite echoes occur even in a dramatic endeavor whose genre made him famous. The influence of *Le Dépit*

---

[4]Lancaster, *French Dramatic Literature*, 1, 109.
[5]*Ibid.*, 2, 617.
[6]Courville, *Luigi Riccoboni dit Lélio*, 1, 66.
[7]McKee, *Theater of Marivaux*, 41.

amoureux will be discussed first, then that of *La Princesse d'Elide,* and finally that of *Le Bourgeois gentilhomme.*

It will be recalled that, in Molière's *Le Dépit amoureux* the origin of the spite originates in Eraste's jealousy, whereas in Marivaux's play, it stems from the reciprocal disdain feigned by both Lélio and the Countess for the opposite sex. Nevertheless, Lélio's own attitude concerning women has been prompted by a fit of jealousy that he experienced in the course of an episode alluded to but not seen in the play, in which he discovered his former mistress' infidelity. Once born, spite will be present in the life of Molière's and Marivaux's characters, and it will give birth to certain similar situations in the development of the two comedies. For example, in both plays there are scenes between valet and master discussing the proper attitude one ought to adopt vis-à-vis women. To arrive at such an attitude, Molière and Marivaux find it necessary to reach a definition for "woman." And in both plays, it is the valet who manages to formulate the definition. Molière has Gros-René put forth the following explanatory label:

> . . . la femme est, comme on dit, mon maître,
> Un certain animal difficile à connaître,
> Et de qui la nature est fort encline au mal.
> Et comme un animal est toujours animal,
> Elle ne sera jamais qu'un animal. (IV, 2)

Likewise, in *La Surprise de l'amour,* Arlequin defines "woman" as "en vérité, c'est pourtant un joli petit animal que cette femme, un joli petit chat; c'est dommage qu'elle ait tant de griffes" (I, 2). Thus the word *animal* is found in both definitions, and it is probable that Marivaux remembered Molière's play in this instance. Such a conclusion is corroborated not only by the similarities pointed to above between the two scenes in question, but also by the end of both scenes that reveals the valets' like attitude toward women. Gros-René declares: "Et moi, je ne veux plus m'embarrasser de femme, / A toutes je renonce" (IV, 2); whereas Arlequin concludes: "Oh! voilà qui est fait! je renonce à toutes les femmes" (I, 2). Here again, worthy of note is the fact that both valets express their thought with the same words arranged differently.

Another situation common to both plays is the quarrel and the reconciliation of the two lovers. Molière's characters speak in the following manner.

> ERASTE: Hé bien! madame, hé bien! . . .
>   Je romps avecque vous, et j'y romps pour jamais . . .
>
> LUCILE: Tant mieux: c'est m'obliger . . .
>
> ERASTE: Que sois-je exterminé, si je ne tiens parole!
>
> LUCILE: Me confonde le ciel, si la mienne est frivole.

ERASTE: Adieu donc.

LUCILE: Adieu donc . . .

ERASTE: . . . cruelle, c'est vous qui l'avez voulu.

LUCILE: Moi? point du tout. C'est vous qui l'avez résolu . . .

ERASTE: Mais si mon coeur encore revoulait sa prison;
      Si, tout fâché qu'il est, il demandait pardon . . . ?
      Je le demande enfin, me l'accorderez-vous,
      Ce pardon obligeant?

LUCILE: Ramenez-moi chez nous. (IV, 3)

and Marivaux's personages bicker in like fashion:

LELIO: Ce voisinage-là me déplaît; je crois que je ferais fort bien de m'en aller,
    dût-elle en penser ce qu'elle voudra . . .

LA COMTESSE: Hélas! Monsieur, je ne vous voyais pas. Après cela, quand je vous
    aurais vu, je ne me ferais pas un grand scrupule d'approcher de l'endroit
    où vous êtes . . . Allez-vous-en donc, ou je m'en vais . . .

LELIO: Adieu donc, Madame, je suis votre serviteur.

LA COMTESSE: Monsieur, je suis votre servante . . .
    Quoi! vous revenez, Monsieur? (II, 7)

Thus the lovers in both scenes simulate a certain amount of scorn for each other, a desire to part and an inability to carry this desire into practice: the couple Eraste-Lucile demonstrated this inability in the scene quoted above; Lélio and the Countess showed it partly in Act II, Scene 7, and even more extensively in Act III, Scene 6. This is not simply a parallel use of the conventional lovers' quarrel, for there are other similarities that confirm Marivaux's reliance on Molière's play. For example, the matter of returning a portrait precipitates the reconciliation in Molière's comedy as well as in Marivaux's play. In *Le Dépit amoureux* Eraste is spiteful enough to declare

Voici votre portrait; il présente à la vue
Cent charmes éclatants dont vous êtes pourvue;
Mais il cache sous eux cent défauts aussi grands
Et c'est un imposteur enfin que je vous rends. (IV, 3)

This motivates Lucile to return the ring Eraste had given her. But when it becomes apparent that the break is definite, there is nothing else to do, of course, but to make up, inasmuch as the two youngsters are in love and cannot bear a separation. Likewise, in Marivaux's play, the Countess is annoyed enough to ask, "C'est mon portrait qu'on m'a dit que vous avez, et je viens vous prier de me le rendre" (III, 6). Lélio is about to return it, but he hesitates, and rather than part with it, he is moved to ask the Countess' forgiveness. "Madame, condamnez-moi, ou faites-moi grâce" (III, 6). The Countess forgives, and the couple is reconciled.

Seconding the principal action of the two plays are the quarrel and the reconciliation of the two valet-soubrette couples, who, in both comedies, copy the moods of their respective masters.

There are even more similarities between *La Surprise de l'amour* and *La Princesse d'Elide*.[8] The Princess, who despises men, is intrigued, to say the least, when Euryale pretends to have the same sentiments for the female sex. She declares, "D'où vient qu'il n'est pas venu jusqu'ici, et qu'il a pris cette autre route quand il m'a vue?" (III, 3). Likewise, when Lélio flees the garden where he meets the Countess, the latter, although she is apparently scornful of men and tries to avoid them, says: *"parlant de Lélio:* Voilà un jeune homme bien sauvage" (I, 6). Certain ideas in the very next scene of Marivaux's play seem to be taken directly from *La Princesse d'Elide*. The Princess words her scorn for love as follows: ."Toutes ces larmes, tous ces soupirs, tous ces hommages, tous ces respects, sont des embûches qu'on tend à notre coeur, et qui souvent l'engagent à commettre des lâchetés. Pour moi, quand je regarde certains exemples, et les bassesses épouvantables où cette passion ravale les personnes sur qui elle étend sa puissance, je sens tout mon coeur qui s'émeut; et je ne puis souffrir qu'une âme, qui fait profession d'un peu de fierté, ne trouve pas une honte horrible à de telles faiblesses" (II, 1). Similarly, Marivaux's countess rejects love and concludes that it is not a sentiment that someone with self-respect ought to have: "Cesser d'avoir de l'amour pour un homme, c'est, à mon compte, connaître sa faute, s'en repentir, en avoir honte, sentir la misère de l'idole qu'on adorait, et rentrer dans le respect qu'une femme se doit à elle-même" (I, 7). Granted that the emphasis is different (the Princess does not speak of *la misère de l'idole qu'on adorait*; she is interested only in herself, in abiding by her Cornelian concept of honor, whereas the Countess is concerned with *l'amant*), Marivaux's imitation in I, 7 does not stop here. The reply of a cousin of the Princess, Cynthie, "Hé! madame, il est de certaines faiblesses qui ne sont point honteuses, et qu'il est beau même d'avoir dans les plus hauts degrés de gloire" (II, 1), is echoed by Colombine in a reply she addresses to the Countess: "Soyons raisonnables; condamnez les amants déloyaux, les conteurs de sornettes, à être jetés dans la rivière une pierre au col, à merveille; enfermez les coquettes entre quatre murailles, fort bien; mais les amants fidèles, dressez-leur de belles et bonnes statues pour encourager le public" (I, 7).

Still another similarity exists. The Princess realizes she is in love with Euryale and she confesses the fact to herself in the following monologue: "De quelle émotion inconnue sens-je mon coeur atteint? Et

[8]In this play, too, women are compared to animals.

quelle inquiétude secrète est venue troubler tout d'un coup la
tranquilité de mon âme? Ne serait-ce point aussi ce qu'on vient de me
dire? et, sans en rien savoir, n'aimerais-je point ce jeune prince? Ah! si
cela était, je serais personne à me désespérer" (IV, 7)! The Countess in
Marivaux's play words the realization of her love for Lélio in very close
fashion:

LA COMTESSE: Colombine!

COLOMBINE: Madame?

LA COMTESSE: Après tout, aurais-tu raison? Est-ce que j'aimerais?

COLOMBINE: Je crois que oui . . .

LA COMTESSE: Non, je n'aime point encore.

COLOMBINE: Vous avez l'équivalent de cela.

LA COMTESSE: Quoi! je pourrais tomber dans ces malheureuses situations, si
    pleines de troubles, d'inquiétudes, de chagrin; moi, moi? Non, Colom-
    bine, cela n'est pas fait encore; je serais au désespoir. (III, 2)

Noteworthy is the fact that the Countess' noun, *désespoir*, reflects the
Princess' verb, *désespérer*.

The climatic scenes in which the characters confess their love also
have points of resemblance. Euryale declares himself first:
"Pardonnez-moi, madame . . . C'est trop vous tenir dans l'erreur; il
faut lever le masque . . . découvrir à vos yeux les véritables sentiments de mon coeur. Je n'ai jamais aimé que vous, et jamais je
n'aimerai que vous" (V, 2). Lélio is less elaborate, but no less
clear: "*A genoux:* Eh bien! Madame, me voilà expliqué . . .
m'entendez-vous . . . mes extravagances ont combattu trop longtemps
contre vous . . . condamnez-moi, ou faits-moi grâce" (III, 6). Thus,
both Euryale and Lélio confess their love first, and both confessions
contain a request for forgiveness.

I should finally mention one similarity between *Le Bourgeois gentilhomme* and *La Surprise de l'amour*. In Molière's play, Cléonte, who
has been rejected by Lucile, denounces the girl to Covielle, who,
encouraged by his master, proceeds to criticize her. However, each
criticism of Covielle is rejected and answered with a praise by Cléonte:

COVIELLE: Elle, monsieur? Voilà une belle mijaurée, une pimpesouée bien bâtie,
    pour vous donner tant d'amour! Je ne lui vois rien que de très médiocre, et
    vous trouverez cent personnes qui seront plus dignes de vous.
    Premièrement, elle a les yeux petits.

CLEONTE: Cela est vrai, elle a les yeux petits, mais elle les a pleins de feu, les plus
    brillants, les plus perçants du monde, les plus touchants qu'on puisse
    voir.

COVIELLE: Elle a la bouche grande.

CLEONTE: Oui; mais on y voit des grâces qu'on ne voit point aux autres bouches; et cette bouche, en la voyant, inspire des désirs, est la plus attrayante, la plus amoureuse du monde.

COVIELLE: Pour sa taille, elle n'est pas grande.

CLEONTE: Non; mais elle est aisée et bien prise.

COVIELLE: Elle affecte une nonchalance dans son parler et dans ses actions.

CLEONTE: Il est vrai; mais elle a grâce à tout cela, et ses manières sont engageantes, ont je ne sais quel charme à s'insinuer dans les coeurs.

COVIELLE: Pour de l'esprit . . .

CLEONTE: Ah! elle en a, Covielle, du plus fin, du plus délicat.

COVIELLE: Sa conversation . . .

CLEONTE: Sa conversation est charmante.

COVIELLE: Elle est toujours sérieuse . . .

CLEONTE: Veux-tu de ces enjouements épanouis, de ces joies toujours ouvertes? et vois-tu rien de plus impertinent que des femmes qui rient à tout propos?

COVIELLE: Mais enfin elle est capricieuse autant que personne au monde.

CLEONTE: Oui, elle est capricieuse, j'en demure d'accord, mais tout sied bien aux belles, on souffre tout des belles. (III, 9)

Finally, Covielle wonders how his master will be able to forget her if he still thinks she is perfect. Cléonte's reply is: "C'est en quoi ma vengeance sera plus éclatante, en quoi je veux faire voir la force de mon coeur à la hair, à la quitter, toute belle, toute pleine d'attraits, toute aimable que je la trouve" (III, 9). Lélio, too, having been rejected, tries to persuade himself and his valet that women are harmful and should be avoided. But in so doing, he only manages to show his inner dependence on the fair sex. What should have been a critical denunciation of "women" becomes a eulogy.

> Femmes, vous nous ravissez notre raison, notre liberté, notre repos; vous nous ravissez à nous-mêmes, et vous nous laissez vivre! Ne voilà-t-il pas des hommes en bel état après? Des pauvres fous, des hommes troublés, ivres de douleur ou de joie, toujours en convulsion, des esclaves! Et à qui appartiennent ces esclaves? A des femmes. . . . car enfin, est-il dans l'univers de figure plus charmante? Que de grâces! et que de variété dans ces grâces? . . . Voyez ses ajustements: jupes étroites, jupes en lanternes, coiffure en clocher, coiffure sur le nez, capuchon sur la tête, et toutes les modes les plus extravagantes: mettez-les sur une femme; dès qu'elles auront touché la figure enchanteresse, c'est l'Amour et les Grâces qui l'ont habillée; c'est de l'esprit qui lui vient jusques au bout des doigts. (I, 2)

And like Cléonte, Lélio also hopes to be able to avoid women in spite of, or perhaps because of, their infinite attractiveness. He replies to Arlequin: "Eh! mon cher Arlequin, me crois-tu plus exempt que toi de ces petites inquiétudes-là? Je me ressouviens qu'il y a des femmes au monde, qu'elles sont aimables, et ce ressouvenir ne va pas, sans

quelques émotions de coeur; mais ce sont ces émotions-là qui me
rendent inébranlable dans la résolution de ne plus voir de femmes" (I,
2). The resemblance between the two scenes under discussion has been
noted by Kenneth N. McKee, summarily, in a footnote, without
elaboration.[9] What might have been pointed out in addition to the
similarities is one rather important difference between Cléonte and
Lélio: the first praises and desires to avoid only one particular woman,
Lucile; whereas Lélio's sentiments, although alike, refer to "women"
in general. Yet, the rapport between the scenes in question cannot be
merely coincidental.

On the basis of the comparisons cited, it is clear, then, that Molière's
influence persisted in *La Surprise de l'amour*. This, of course, does not
detract from the ease with which Marivaux's pen moves in this comedy;
the turn of his phrase is highly polished, great variety of feelings is
expressed by his characters, and all the subtle nuances of thought and
emotion that Marivaux's *aficionados* find exeedingly attractive are
present throughout. Typical eighteenth-century sophisticated badinage, fatuous though it may be at times, and so uncharacteristic of
the directness of Molière, succeeds, under Marivaux's guidance, in
dissecting and then refining the gradations of human sentiments that
constitute the trademark of the eighteenth-century playwright. The
basis of this trademark is, of course, *la surprise de l'amour*, a constant
in Marivaux's dramatic compositions. The presence of a constant,
however, has come under attack, for it has been held that it provides too
much anticipatory prowess for spectators and readers, that it tends to
foster monotony, and that, in fact, the *surprise* provides for no surprise
at all. The first who opted for such an interpretation was the Marquis
d'Argens, who wrote, "Il y a dans ses pièces, d'ailleurs très jolies, un
défaut, c'est qu'elles pourraient être presque toutes intitulées *La Surprise de l'amour*."[10] Numerous critics have adopted this point of view
since, yet admirers of Marivaux interpret it as a misconception. The
fact is that Marivaux himself, having heard this criticism with his own
ears, attempted to reject it. According to D'Alembert's report, his
friend defended himself as follows: "J'ai guetté dans le coeur humain
toutes les niches différentes où peut se cacher l'amour lorsqu'il craint
de se montrer, et chacune de mes comédies a pour objet de le faire
sortir d'une de ses niches."[11] Obviously Marivaux took the criticism to
heart, for he wrote further in the *Avertissement* of *Les Serments indiscrets*
that in his plays "tout se passe dans le coeur; mais ce coeur a bien des

[9]McKee, *Theater of Marivaux*, 31.
[10]Marquis d'Argens, *Réflexions historiques et critiques sur le goût* (Paris: Marquis d'Argens,
1743), 233.
[11]Quoted in Marivaux, *Théâtre*, vol. 1 (Paris: Editions Dort, 1961), 1, i.

sortes de sentiments, et le portrait de l'un ne fait pas le portrait de l'autre." Théophile Gautier contrasts such a procedure with that usually employed by Molière.

> Chez Marivaux, on commence à sentir le véritable coeur humain. A travers mille fanfreluches coquettes, on découvre quelque chose de bien nouveau pour le temps, l'analyse sérieuse de l'amour. Molière, qui excellait dans la peinture des caractères en toute autre chose, n'avait fait vibrer qu'une seule fois cette corde-là, dans *Le Misanthrope;* autrement ses amoureux sont de simples jeunes premiers, n'émettant que des sentiments traditionnels et se ressemblant tous. Ce sont les Pamphile et les Chéréas de la comédie latine — des amoureux si l'on veut, des gens qui aiment, jamais.[12]

Although Théophile Gautier's reputation, in the main, is not that of a literary critic, it is interesting to note Gustave Larroumet's conclusion in this context.

> S'il se contente de fouiller les cachettes du coeur, il est rare qu'il n'en trouve pas de nouvelles. Chacune de ses tentatives est marquée par une découverte qui a toujours son prix; il n'est pas une de ses pièces, bonne ou médiocre, qui n'apprenne quelque chose sur la manière dont l'amour naît ou meurt. N'est-ce point là une suffisante nouveauté, et, au lieu de reprocher à Marivaux une stérile ressemblance dans les sujets qu'il traite, ne conviendrait-il pas d'admirer plutôt avec quelle souplesse il varie, au point de la transformer chaque fois, une situation dont le point de départ est, en effet, toujours le même?[13]

Thus, it appears that originality and imitation blend in *La Surprise de l'amour* and result in a comedy that does honor both to the eighteenth-century playwright and to his illustrious predecessor whose own inventiveness supports and reinforces that of Marivaux.

---

[12]Théophile Gautier, *Histoire de l'art dramatique* (Paris: Magnin, Blanchard et Cie, 1858), 5, 292.

[13]Larroumet, *Marivaux, sa vie et ses oeuvres,* 182-183.

LE DENOUEMENT IMPREVU

Although by 1724 Marivaux had had a number of successes at the Théâtre Italien, his only tragedy, *Annibal*, had failed at the Théâtre Français in 1720, and the dramatist aspired to have another shot at fame by earning the appreciation of the more sophisticated audiences that frequented the Théâtre Français. The acclaim of the Théâtre Italien could not by itself consecrate an author, whereas success at the Théâtre Français usually meant an unerasable stamp of approval. According to Fournier and Bastide, because of his successes elsewhere, "les comédiens français avaient demandé une pièce à Marivaux qui, pour aller plus vite, leur promit seulement un acte: ce fut *Le Dénouement imprévu*."[1] The play was presented as a curtain raiser to *Le Jaloux désabusé* by Campistron. Success, however, in the house of Molière, was not easy to come by, for although *Le Mercure de France* described Marivaux's comedy as one "pleine d'esprit, et fort bien écrite," it also added that "elle n'a pas eu beaucoup de succès."[2] No critic at the time, and only one since,[3] saw similarities between *Le Dénouement imprévu* and Molière's plays, and perhaps the failure can be explained by the fact that a Molière-tuned audience was naturally unable to find to its liking stage episodes that it could not associate with those with which it was most familiar. In this context, it is interesting to note that, although Marivaux was thwarted at every turn in so far as success at the Théâtre Français was concerned, today his comedies rank second in frequency of performance only to those of Molière. There are surely many reasons for this, but one may be the vogue of the *rapprochement* between marivaldian and *moliéresque* themes.

The subject of *Le Dénouement imprévu* lends itself to a comparison with certain well-known themes of Molière. Monsieur Argante has decided to marry his daughter to a man she has never met, Eraste. Her boyfriend, Dorante, appeals more to her, although she does not love him; he simply represents security, for she knows him, and would prefer to be able to anticipate a mediocre existence than to wonder about one with which she is entirely unfamiliar. In order to prevent, or postpone at least, the projected marriage with Eraste, she is persuaded by boyfriend, maid, and others in her entourage to display a certain amount of mental aberration, and thereby discourage the unknown suitor. The unforeseen, however, occurs when Eraste and

---

[1] Jean Fournier and Maurice Bastide, eds., *Théâtre Complet de Marivaux* (Paris: Les Editions Nationales, 1946), 1, 208.
[2] *Le Mercure de France* (Paris), December 1724, pp. 2862-2863.
[3] Greene, *Marivaux*, 89; but he only devotes one line to the comparison.

Mademoiselle Argante meet, and an instantaneous sparkle of love puts an end to the maiden's rebellion and confirms the paternally desired *dénouement*. A celebration, complete with musicians and promises of eternal joy, fills the not-so-surprising ending of the play.

Certain facets of the plot immediately bring to mind a number of scenes from *Le Tartuffe* and from *Monsieur de Pourceaugnac*. It will be recalled that, in *Le Tartuffe*, Marianne has just been advised by her father that she is to marry Tartuffe, and Dorine is angry that her mistress did not show enough opposition.

> . . . Je vois que vous voulez
> Etre à monsieur Tartuffe; et j'aurais, quand j'y pense,
> Tort de vous détourner d'une telle alliance . . .
> Il a l'oreille rouge et le teint bien fleuri;
> Vous vivrez trop contente avec un tel mari . . .
> Votre sort est fort beau: de quoi vous plaignez-vous?
> Vous irez par la coche en sa petite ville,
> Qu'en oncles et cousins vous trouverez fertile,
> Et vous vous plairez fort à les entretenir,
> D'abord chez le beau monde on vous fera venir.
> Vous irez visiter, pour votre bienvenue,
> Madame la baillive et madame l'élue,
> Qui d'un siège pliant vous feront honorer.
> Là, dans le carnaval. . . . (II, 3)

The situation in Marivaux's play is similar: Mademoiselle Argante has just been told that she is to marry Eraste instead of Dorante. As in *Le Tartuffe*, the servant, Lisette, tries to convince the young girl to outwit her father. Lisette's arguments are the same as those of Dorine: in a highly sarcastic manner, she praises Eraste and the kind of life her mistress will have with him in order to persuade her that a less scrupulous opposition to the marriage in question is in order.

> Je crois qu'effectivement vous avez raison. Il vaut mieux que vous épousiez ce jeune rustre que nous attendons. Que de repos vous allez avoir à sa campagne! Plus de toilette, plus de miroir, plus de boîte à mouches; cela ne rapporte rien. Ce n'est pas comme à Paris. . . . C'est un embarras que tout cela, et on ne l'a pas à la campagne: il n'y a pas là que de . . . bon appétit. . . . J'oubliais le meilleur. Vous aurez parfois des galants hobereaux qui viendront vous rendre hommage . . . vous irez vous promener avec eux. . . . Prenez votre parti, sinon je recommence, et je vous nomme tous les animaux de votre ferme, jusqu'à votre mari. (Scene 4)

The method of attack is comparable: Dorine refers to the appetite of Tartuffe in *Il a l'oreille rouge et le teint bien fleuri*; Lisette says, *Il n'y a pas là que de . . . bon appétit*; Dorine mentions the *petite ville* of Tartuffe; Lisette satirizes the *jeune rustre* and his *campagne*; Dorine anticipates with irony the entertaining Marianne will have to do in: *vous vous plairez fort à les entretenir*; and Lisette foresees with sarcasm: *Vous aurez parfois des galants hobereaux qui viendront vous rendre hommage*

. . . *vous irez vous promener avec eux;* finally, Dorine speaks of *le carnaval* in which Marianne will have to live; and Lisette mentions the *hobereaux*[4] and *tous les animaux de votre ferme*.

There is also a notable similarity between *Le Dénouement imprévu* and *Monsieur de Pourceaugnac*. In Moliere's play, Julie meets Monsieur de Pourceaugnac and flirts with him in a manner deliberately designed to disgust and scare away the future husband. "Ah! le voilà sans doute, et mon coeur me le dit. Qu'il est bien fait! qu'il a bon air! et que je suis contente d'avoir un tel époux! Souffrez que je l'embrasse, et que je lui témoigne . . . que je suis aise de vous voir! et que je brûle d'impatience . . . [To her father] Ne voulez-vous pas que je caresse l'époux que vous m'avez choisi?" (II, 6). Similarly, in Marivaux's play Mademoiselle Argante meets Eraste, and with the same calculated deliberation, she puts on the mask of a coquette: "Sait-il aimer? a-t-il des sentiments, de la figure? est-il grand, est-il petit?" (Scene 2). Her questions are not so daring as the unchecked exclamations of Julie; nevertheless they are flirtatious in type, and they too are destined to scare the future husband away.

These similarities notwithstanding, Marivaux attempts to change, somewhat, the character of his personages, if not the situations themselves. In Scene 4, for example, Lisette is much less cruel than Dorine: she does not cause Mademoiselle Argante to say, "Ah! tu me fais mourir!" as Dorine does to Marianne. In Scene 11, Mademoiselle Argante does not dare to be as impudent as Julie; her tone is milder, her behavior more tamed. In fact, before the scene is over, she asks Eraste: "Que ne vous ai-je connu plutôt? . . . Est-il possible que je vous aie haï?"

About Mademoiselle Argante's quick admission that she is in love with Eraste, it has been said that the "ending was not only *imprévu;* it was precipitous! And herein lies the weakness of the play."[5] This observation also has been applied to many of Molière's endings, and it is not perhaps unfruitful to remark that quick and unexpected endings are often used by Marivaux in the very plays where other *moliéresque* influences are noted.[6]

Le Dénouement imprévu has numerous other sources as well. Chief among these is Regnard's *Les Folies amoureuses*. Gustave Larroumet,[7] for example, observed that Scene 7 of Marivaux's play is an imitation of

---

[4]Although the secondary meaning of this word is *gentilhommes campagnards*, its primary meaning is *petits faucons, genre d'oiseaux rapaces*.

[5]McKee, *Theater of Marivaux*, 76.

[6]See, for example, the ending of *Arlequin poli par l'amour, L'Héritier de village, Les Sincères,* and *Félicie*.

[7]Larroumet, *Marivaux, sa vie et ses oeuvres*, 156.

Act II, Scene 6 of Regnard's comedy: both Agathe and Mademoiselle
Argante pretend to have become demented in order to avoid a marriage
with someone they do not love; both girls manifest their state by wearing
extravagant clothes and by playing an instrument. Jean Fleury[8] and E.
J. H. Greene[9] maintain that the gardener, Pierre, is but an imitation of
his counterpart in Dufresny's play *L'Esprit de contradiction*. However,
neither critic offers any proof, and a close reading of the text in question
does not reveal specific similarities between the two characters. There
is rather an imitation of the gardener in Dancourt's *Les Vendanges de
Surennes:* both pretend to govern their respective master (Scene 1 in
both plays); both report to their respective master the conversation
between the master's daughter and her respective *amant* (Scene 1 in
Dancourt's comedy, Scene 2 in Marivaux's); finally, the language the
gardeners use in the two situations mentioned is similar, although
contained in speeches too long to cite here.

In spite of the reminiscences, and occasional instances of outright
imitation, *Le Dénouement imprévu* contains typically marivaldian
lines. Consider, for example, Mademoiselle Argante's words to her
father: "Vous êtes le maître, *distinguo*: pour les choses raisonnables,
oui; pour celles qui ne le sont pas, non. On ne force point les coeurs.
Loi établie. Vous voulez forcer le mien: vous transgressez la loi. J'ai de
la vertu, je la veux garder. Si j'épousais votre magot, que deviendrait-
elle? Je n'en sais rien" (Scene 7). The kind of rebellion found both in
Regnard and Molière is absent from Marivaux's episode, which uses,
instead, lively, impertinent satire of a type that was more appropriate
for the Théâtre Français than for the stage of Le Théâtre Italien with
which the playwright was more familiar. Consider, also, the following
bit of dialogue that expresses *la surprise de l'amour* when Mademoiselle
Argante and Eraste meet.

> ERASTE [*à part*]: Ah! L'aimable personne! pourquoi l'ai-je vue, puisque je dois
> la perdre?
> MADEMOISELLE ARGANTE [*à part, en entrant*]: Voilà un joli homme! Si Eraste lui
> ressemblait, je ne ferais pas la folle. (Scene 11)

The immediate enlightenment caused by awakened love has both
protagonists open their hearts within a matter of minutes in order to
utter a refreshing expression of love that pours unchecked before the
audience has had a chance to catch its breath. There is impulse, of
course, in all this, and more of an outline than depth. Yet, profundity
often must be summarily stated, and if Marivaux directs his play along
lines other than those that his spectators could aniticipate, it must be

[8]Fleury, *Marivaux et le marivaudage*, 106.
[9]Greene, *Marivaux*, 89.

considered to his credit that, for once, *la surprise de l'amour* does indeed provide for surprise. It is difficult to understand why Jean Fleury, in commenting upon the lack of success of *Le Dénouement imprévu* at the Théâtre Français, declared that "Il n'est permis qu'à Corneille de nous imposer de ces surprises."[10] Obviously, in the early eighteenth century, newcomers at the Théâtre Français were not accorded the same privileges as those enjoyed by established classics. This, too, explains the failure of *Le Dénouement imprévu*. Sprinkled here and there though it was with *moliéresque* and other recollections, unperceived by Marivaux's contemporaries, the play failed; for present-day literary historians, however, *Le Dénouement imprévu* is still another interesting example of how questionable is D'Alembert's report of Marivaux's alleged dislike for Molière.

[10]Fleury, *Marivaux et le marivaudage*, 105.

L'HERITIER DE VILLAGE

Although he was an experienced writer by 1725 when *L'Héritier de village* was first presented at the Théâtre Italien, Marivaux's eleventh play is generally considered to be one of the least original of his repertory. His sole excursion into peasant society, and one of the few of his social plays, appears to have been in need of a variety of sources that the playwright found in a number of comedies on similar topics and, of course, in at least two of Molière's plays, *Georges Dandin* and *Le Bourgeois gentilhomme*.

The plot of *L'Héritier de village* revolves around a peasant, Blaise, who inherits unexpectedly a considerable amount of money and, of course, acquires at the same time an invincible taste for nobility. Putting on the airs of an aristocrat, he hires a tutor for his children, Arlequin, and he attempts to have his offspring marry into the local aristocracy. Moreover, he advises his wife to take on at least thirty lovers, and is himself eager to get a mistress. His social climbing is replete with an entire gamut of gaucheries. He refuses pompously to pay his debts, for a rich man must insist that creditors make repeated demands before they are paid; he admits to the village tax collector that he owes him money, but refuses to pay because an aristocrat simply does not discharge his fiscal responsibilities; he declares that his wife's lovers will cause him no concern because *gens de qualité* are not supposed to be jealous; and he begins to look back nostalgically to his less complex past, to the happy people who have no great affairs to manage and therefore enjoy a tranquility that is now lost for him. At the end of the play word is received happily that the notary of the family has disappeared with the money, and Blaise, wife, and children will revert to the more crude and more blissful state of poverty from which they had been temporarily exiled.

J. A. Desboulmiers called *L'Héritier de village* "une mauvaise copie de *L'Usurier gentilhomme*."[1] Legrand's comedy, presented in 1712, and with which Marivaux might have been familiar, has, in fact, nothing in common with *L'Héritier de village*. Its plot resembles only remotely that of Marivaux, on a general level, and its various scenes differ entirely from the episodes of Marivaux's choice. Jean Fleury remarked that "Il faut beaucoup de bonne volonté pour trouver du rapport entre ces deux comédies. . . . Il n'y a donc aucune comparaison à établir entre les deux pièces."[2] It is curious that an

---

[1] J. A. Desboulmiers, *Histoire anecdotique et raisonnée du Théâtre Italien depuis son rétablissement en France jusqu'à l'année 1769* (Paris: Lacombe, 1769), 2, 413.

[2] Fleury, *Marivaux et le marivaudage*, 109.

eighteenth-century critic specified inexistent similarities between
L'Héritier de village and another play; yet close as he was to the theater
of Molière, he did not mention any possible influence of *Le Bourgeois
gentilhomme*, which is at the basis of so many of the social plays of the
time that satirize the practice of social climbing. Kenneth N. McKee
himself calls *L'Héritier de village* a *dancourade*, and devotes only two
lines to the *moliéresque* influence;[3] and E. J. H. Greene contents
himself with saying that *L'Héritier de village* "resembles a run-of-the-
mill comedy of manners."[4] On the contrary, Gustave Larroumet wrote,
"*L'Héritier de village* rappelle à chaque instant *Georges Dandin* et *Le
Bourgeois gentilhomme*."[5]

To begin with, at least one comparison can be made between
Marivaux's play and Molière's *Georges Dandin*. It will be recalled that
in the latter comedy, one reads of the considerable concern of Monsieur
and Madame de Sotenville about the way in which Georges Dandin,
who, likewise, has married into the local aristocracy, addresses them.

> MADAME DE SOTENVILLE: Ne vous déférez-vous jamais, avec moi, de la familarité
> de ce mot de ma bellemère, et ne sauriez-vous vous accoutumer à me
> dire madame?

> MONSIEUR DE SOTENVILLE: Doucement, mon gendre. Apprenez qu'il n'est pas
> respectueux d'appeler les gens par leur nom, et qu'à ceux qui sont
> au-dessus de nous il faut dire monsieur tout court.

> GEORGES DANDIN: Hé bien! monsieur tout court, et non plus monsieur de Soten-
> ville. (I, 4)

In various parts of Marivaux's play, one also finds a similar concern
over the proper way of addressing the *gens de qualité*, for example, the
description made by Blaise to his wife as to how they should conduct
themselves from now on: "Je te connais, je vians à toi, et je batifole
dans le discours; je te dis . . . Madame par-ci, Madame par-là" (Scene
2). In addition, Blaise's wife, Claudine, after finding out that her
husband has inherited one hundred thousand francs, demands that the
Chevalier show her proper respect: "Boutez-vous à votre devoir, hon-
orez ma personne, traitez-moi de Madame, demandez-moi comment se
porte ma santé, mettez au bout quelque coup de chapiau" (Scene 3).
And in the very next scene the Chevalier agrees with the demands of
Blaise and of Claudine, just like Georges Dandin above — although for
different reasons[6]— and addresses them as well as their children in the

---

[3]McKee, *Theater of Marivaux*, 86-87.
[4]Greene, *Marivaux*, 97.
[5]Larroumet, *Marivaux, sa vie et ses oeuvres*, 156.
[6]Georges Dandin agrees in order to avoid the interruptions of his in-laws; the Chevalier agrees
for monetary reasons.

proper way: *Monsieur, je suis votre serviteur, je vous fais réparation; Messieurs vos enfants; Monsieur et Madame Blaise* (Scene 4).

There is, however, a notable difference between the character of Georges Dandin and that of Blaise. From the very beginning and throughout the play, Molière has his hero express extreme regret that he has married into a *famille de qualité* and tried to become *un homme de qualité*: "Que mon mariage est une leçon bien parlante à tous les paysans qui veulent s'élever au-dessus de leur condition. . . . Georges Dandin! Georges Dandin! vous avez fait une sottise, la plus grande du monde. Ma maison est effroyable maintenant et je n'y rentre point sans y trouver quelque chagrin" (I, 1). Later he declares: "L'égalité de condition laisse du moins à l'honneur d'un mari la liberté du ressentiment. . . . Mais vous avez voulu tâter de la noblesse . . . je me donnerais volontiers des souflets" (I, 3). The tears of this sincerely repentant man do not stop here. He cries, "Vous l'avez voulu, Georges Dandin, vous l'avez voulu" (I, 9). And finally: "Je n'y vois plus de remède. Lorsqu'on a, comme moi, épousé une méchante femme, le meilleur parti qu'on puisse prendre, c'est de s'aller jeter dans l'eau, la tête la première" (III, 15). On the contrary, in Marivaux's play, Blaise is never sorry *de brûler l'étape*. Nobility inspires him to adopt the questionable manners practiced by the Parisian dandies of the day: "Il faut se conduire à l'aise, avoir une vertu négligeante, se permettre un maintien commode, qui ne soit point malhonnête, qui ne soit point honnête non plus" (Scene 2). Nobility also inspires in Blaise aims that Georges Dandin constantly tries to eliminate from his own household. Thus, Blaise does not consider it proper to love his wife any more: "Nous aimer, femme! il faut bien s'en garder; vraiment, ça jetterait un biau cotton dans le monde!" (Scene 2); he desires to acquire a mistress: "Il y a une autre bagatelle qui est encore pour le bon air, c'est que j'aurons une maîtresse" (Scene 2); and he wants his wife to surround herself with several *galants:* "Je te varrions un régiment de galants à l'entour de toi . . . T'en auras trente, et non pas un" (Scene 2).

Thus, it might be said that *Georges Dandin* is a continuation of *L'Héritier de village;* in other words, Georges Dandin suffers the consequences of his fortune and of marrying outside his class, whereas Blaise, who is about to share Georges Dandin's fate, is saved by the loss of his money. Outside the basic situation of a social climber (which was common to many plays of the time) and the rapports cited, Blaise and Georges Dandin do not have enough in common to validate completely the first part of Gustave Larroumet's statement quoted above.

The second part of the statement is, however, valid, for there are a number of varied similarities between *L'Héritier de village* and *Le Bourgeois gentilhomme*. To begin with, Monsieur Jourdain is preoccupied with the necessity of having servants just to be *à la mode des gens de qualité,* not because he really needs them.

MONSIEUR JOURDAIN: Laquais! holà, mes deux laquais!

PREMIER LAQUAIS: Que voulez-vous, monsieur?

MONSIEUR JOURDAIN: Rien. C'est pour voir si vous m'entendez bien. (I, 2)

Similarly, in Marivaux's comedy, as soon as Blaise has inherited the money and returned to his village, he proceeds to hire a servant for like reasons.

BLAISE: Eh! eh! baille-moi cinq sous de mornaie, te disje.

CLAUDINE: Pourquoi donc, Nicodème?

BLAISE: Pour ce garçon qui apporte mon paquet depis la voiture jusqu'à chez nous, pendant que je marchais tout bellement et à mon aise . . .

CLAUDINE: Et tu dépenses cinq sous en porteux de paquets?

BLAISE: Oui, par magière de récréation. (Scene 1)

It will be recalled that Monsieur Jourdain is interested in the type of clothing worn by the nobility.

LE MAITRE TAILLEUR: Tenez, voilà le plus bel habit de la cour, et le mieux assorti. C'est un chef-d'oeuvre . . .

MONSIEUR JOURDAIN: Qu'est-ce que c'est que ceci? vous avez mis les fleurs en en bas.

LE MAITRE TAILLEUR: Vous ne m'avez pas dit que vous les vouliez en en haut.

MONSIEUR JOURDAIN: Est-ce qu'il faut dire cela?

LE MAITRE TAILLEUR: Oui, vraiment. Toutes les personnes de qualité les portent de la sorte.

MONSIEUR JOURDAIN: Les personnes de qualité portent les fleurs en en bas?

LE MAITRE TAILLEUR: Oui, monsieur.

MONSIEUR JOURDAIN: Oh! voilà qui est donc bien . . . vous avez bien fait. (II, 7)

Likewise, Blaise and Claudine are preoccupied with the kind of clothing that befits their new place in society.

CLAUDINE: Il n'y a d'abord qu'à m'habiller de brocard, acheter des jouyaux et un collier de parles; tu feras pour toi à l'avenant.

BLAISE: Le brocard, les parles et les jouyaux ne font rian à mon dire, t'en auras à bauge, j'aurons itou du d'or sur mon habit.[7] J'avons déjà acheté un castor avec un casquin de friperie, que je bouterons en attendant que j'ayons tout mon équipage à forfait. (Scene 2)

In addition, both plays show the mania of showing off by means of lending money to flatterers. Madame Jourdain protests: "Oui, il a des

[7]The phrase *du d'or sur mon habit* echoes *Le Misanthrope,* where Basque says: "Il porte une jaquette à grand'basques plissées, avec du d'or dessus" (II, 6).

bontés pour vous, et vous fait des caresses; mais il vous emprunte votre argent" (III, 3). Whereupon Monsieur Jourdain answers: "Hé bien! ne m'est-ce pas de l'honneur, de prêter mon argent à un homme de cette condition-là? et puis-je faire moins pour un seigneur qui m'appelle son cher ami?" (III, 3). Blaise cannot resist flattery either:

> Le Fiscal: Vous avez l'âme belle, et j'ai une grâce à vous demander, qui est de vouloir bien me prêter cinquante francs.
>
> Blaise: Tenez, fiscal, je sis ravi de vous sarvir; prenez. (Scene 7)

Moreover, Monsieur Jourdain and Blaise share an equal interest in the necessity of acquiring and spending money for a mistress. Monsieur Jourdain declares: "Il n'y a point de dépense que je ne fisse, si par là je pouvais trouver le chemin de son coeur. Une femme de qualité a pour moi des charmes ravissants; et c'est un honneur que j'achèterais au prix de toutes choses" (III, 6). Likewise, Blaise reasons: "Une autre bagatelle qui est encore pour le bon air c'est que j'aurons une maîtresse qui sera queuque chiffon de femme, qui sera bian laide, et bian sotte, qui ne m'aimera point, que je n'aimerai point non pus; qui me fera des niches, mais qui me coûtera biaucoup, et qui ne vaura guère, et c'est là le pasisir" (Scene 2). However, Marivaux draws a different comic effect from Blaise's speech; Blaise speaks as a peasant would, his reasoning is practical even though the conclusion, *et c'est là le pasisir*, is debatable. And herein lies the difference between Blaise and Monsieur Jourdain: the first represents a peasant social climber, the second symbolizes the Parisian bourgeois who aspires to a position in the upper classes. It is also clear that, unlike Monsieur Jourdain, Blaise sees the absolute futility of having a mistress, although he will have one because his new position in society requires it. In this sense, Blaise has more logic than Monsieur Jourdain (he is able to anticipate what having a mistress will mean), and yet his character is more paradoxical because he will have a mistress despite his anticipations (whereas Monsieur Jourdain will have one because he can only foresee the advantages and none of the shortcomings of a mistress).

A final resemblance remains to be pointed out between the scene in which Monsieur Jourdain declares his will in regard to the marriage of his daughter, and the one in *L'Héritier de village* in which Blaise gives his approval of the Chevalier and of Madame Damis as son-in-law and daughter-in-law, respectively. Monsieur Jourdain declares: "J'ai du bien assez pour ma fille; je n'ai besoin que d'honneurs, et je la veux faire marquise . . . ma fille sera marquise en dépit de tout le monde; et si vous me mettez en colère, je la ferai duchesse" (III, 12). Acting in order to satisfy his own wish for nobility, Blaise, like Monsieur Jourdain, does not mind paying for his desire: "Touchez là, mon gendre; allons, ma bru, ça vaut fait; j'achèterons de la noblesse" (Scene 5).

It is clear, then, that *L'Héritier de village* is not devoid of a number of *moliéresque* recollections that Marivaux, consciously or not, employed directly or indirectly, sometimes changing and at other times maintaining the emphasis placed on the various episodes by his predecessor. If Desboulmiers failed to notice Molière's influence, it is not because it is not present, rather, perhaps, because he was too close in time to perceive it clearly. If twentieth-century critics such as Kenneth N. McKee and E. J. H. Greene chose to deemphasize the sources Marivaux found in the seventeenth-century playwright, it is not because these sources are unimportant, rather, perhaps, because the critics recall too readily D'Alembert's reports, and because of the tradition among *aficionados* of Marivaux to see in him more originality than he indeed had. In point of fact, a knowledge of the exact sources, of their extent, and of the specific manipulation of each enhances one's appreciation of Marivaux and adds new dimensions to his play-writing abilities. Typical of the unwillingness of some to associate Molière with Marivaux are such uncorroborated assertions as: "Since the eighteenth century, it [*L'Héritier de village*] has suffered by the inevitable comparison with *Le Bourgeois gentilhomme* and *Georges Dandin*";[8] or "Ce [*L'Héritier de village*] n'est au vrai qu'une petite farce, un lever de rideau, qu'écrase le souvenir de *Georges Dandin* et du *Bourgeois gentilhomme*. Marivaux avait plus d'une raison de n'aimer point Molière: chaque fois qu'il le rappelle, il en souffre."[9] As a matter of fact, some of the most boisterous comedy one finds in Marivaux occurs precisely in those passages that are partly or totally inspired by Molière. If *L'Héritier de village* has any merit at all, it is because of the laughter-causing ingredients that the eighteenth-century playwright inserted in those *moliéresque* episodes cited above. The others are indeed run-of-the-mill, slow-moving, monotonous.

Unlike Molière, who had traveled through the provinces and had gotten to know the peasants well, Marivaux's social acquaintances were mostly Parisian. He was always more adept in describing the powdered and bewigged aristocrats of Parisian drawing rooms than in portraying the peasants and their problems. True, the playwright would once in a while sojourn in the country. But then this kind of outing almost always had a castle as its destination, and if he observed the peasants at all, it was from a distance, making it impossible for him to become aware of the suffering and injustice with which the lords harnessed them. His

[8]Greene, *Marivaux*, 99.
[9]Arland, *Marivaux*, 142.

direct knowledge of the peasantry was limited to observing those members of the class who served the owners of the castle in which he resided. And these were the well-off members, the mild and the domesticated ones who enjoyed the security of food and shelter. If they differed at all from the masters, it was only in dress, in speech, and perhaps in their naïveté. The Blaise of *L'Héritier de village* could not possibly stem from the author's direct vision; he had to be, in the more amusing scenes in which one finds him, a character built according to the literary recollections of the playwright. It is to Marivaux's credit, then, that instead of depicting a personage of whom he had little first-hand knowledge, he used instead (to a certain extent), the available cupboard of *moliéresque* types and techniques. Still, perhaps because Marivaux's imitation is limited, his hero lacks the involvement of feelings one notes in Georges Dandin, and he cannot become immersed in any real kind of crisis. Not even when news of the loss of his money reaches him is he unduly saddened, and in fact he appears rather relieved. Neither he nor any member of his family is distressed at any time. Distress there is, of course, in some of the minor characters such as the Chevalier and Madame Damis, who submit to all sorts of humiliations in order to partake of the fortune of the peasant. Their situation is akin to that of a crisis, yet none of the main characters ever suffers or cries. E. J. H. Greene is correct when he writes: "Herein lies the weakness of the play. It is not that it has any glaring defects, or that it is poorly constructed. But there is something important missing, something we expect even in the slightest of Marivaux's comedies, even (or especially) in a critical comedy, and that is . . . [that] the spectator can neither identify himself with certain characters and share their emotions, nor can he enjoy the pleasure of seeing the wicked and the irresponsible get what they deserve."[10] What all this seems to imply, however, is that Marivaux erred in not making of Blaise a more faithful copy of Georges Dandin, who does suffer, does cry, and does indeed find himself in a continuous state of crisis without exit, without solution. Had he merely reiterated the theme of social climbing within a more immediately recognizable *moliéresque* format rather than simply recollecting only certain scenes, he might have been able to elicit a better reception. As it was, however, having visualized *L'Héritier de village* as a continuation of *Georges Dandin*,[11] dotted here and there with limited episodes from *Le Bourgeois gentilhomme*, his play had, initially, only a six-day run, and hardly ever has been presented since.

[10]Greene, *Marivaux*, 99.
[11]See above discussion.

L'ILE DE LA RAISON

Two years after *L'Héritier de village,* Marivaux composed a philosophical comedy the subtitle of which was *Les Petits hommes,* and which he read at first in a number of Parisian drawing rooms where it received a great deal of applause. In addition to the material one had come to expect of the author, the listeners must have enjoyed the sophisticated language of the characters, language that they could recognize, but above all they must have been taken in by the ingenious idea of devising a play around a theme popular at the time, namely that of Lilliputianism, which stemmed from a current translation of *Gulliver's Travels.* The reading of *L'Ile de la raison* was extremely popular, because the listeners could give free rein to their imagination, and the changing size of the characters did not constitute an impediment to enjoyment. Its success in the drawing rooms prompted the Comédie Française to include Marivaux's comedy in its repertory, particularly since they had accepted previously *La (Seconde) Surprise de l'amour,*[1] the presentation of which had to be postponed for many months because of difficulties over casting and production. Marivaux, who was eager to have another shot at the Théâtre Français, gave his approval without anticipating that the bizarre events in the play would be most difficult to stage. *L'Ile de la raison* failed in spite of or because of considerable public expectation, for size transformations, which can be easily imagined by readers, could not materialize successfully in front of the spectators' eyes. Verisimilitude was constrained, illusion was lost, and the pungency of the lines evaporated for an audience attempting to reconcile fact with imagination. The *Mercure de France* stated, "Quoique pleine d'esprit, [the play] n'a pas été goûtée du public."[2] To counteract the review of the *Mercure,* Marivaux wrote what became a much discussed prologue that may have been inspired by Dufresny's *Le Double veuvage.*[3] The prologue is, in effect, an apology for the play in which the writer anticipates possible criticism and attempts to answer it. His effort notwithstanding, *L'Ile de la raison* was *magnifiquement sifflée* in the course of the first night, and was dropped after the fourth performance. In spite of its lack of success, however, the Théâtre Italien adapted most of the ideas of the playwright for their own version of the comedy that they entitled *L'Ile de la folie.* This version had a respectable, well-attended seventeen-day run barely two weeks after its withdrawal from the repertory of the Théâtre Français.

[1]More about which in the following chapter.
[2]*Le Mercure de France* (Paris), September 1727, p. 2087.
[3]See Fleury, *Marivaux et le marivaudage,* 89, and McKee, *Theater of Marivaux,* 91.

Yet *L'Ile de la raison,* overlooked in the eighteenth and nineteenth century, was revived in Paris by an avant-garde group in 1950. The skillful director of the Compagnie de L'Equipe diminished the lack of verisimilitude of the play by devising a platform on which he placed the islanders, whose size was normal, and a concealed trough in front of it, from which those of lesser stature could be raised or lowered in order to give to spectators the illusion of growing and shrinking that the playwright required. Such devices have been used with such success each time that *L'Ile de la raison* was revived that, today, there is little doubt that the comedy is playable on the stage and indeed worthy of production. This, to Marivaux's dismay, was not the case at the time. Although both *Gulliver's Travels* and *Le Double veuvage* enjoyed a considerable measure of popularity with the public, his failure may be attributed once more, in part, to the failure of his contemporaries to see in it *moliéresque* themes that, if noted, would have placed them on more familiar territory. Surprisingly, not only were the eighteenth-century audiences shortsighted, but even later reviewers and critics failed to associate *L'Ile de la raison* with any Molière play.

Yet, several instances in Marivaux's comedy smack of the influence of his predecessor. The plot, even cursorily reviewed, ought to provide some immediate hints. It centers around the idea that the size of human beings changes in proportion to their reasonableness: they become taller when they exhibit *bon sens,* and they shrink as they abandon themselves to ungenerous, uncivilized, and prejudice-filled conduct. The action takes place on an island, the natives of which are all rational beings of normal size. Following a shipwreck, eight Europeans are brought to the mythical place in question: the Courtier, his secretary, Frontignac, the Countess, her chambermaid, Spinette, a poet, a philosopher, a doctor, and a peasant. Upon arrival, the stature of each changes in accordance with his particular state of irrationality at the time. Marivaux is audacious enough (for the eighteenth century) to describe the size of the peasant, Blaise, as having changed least of all, for his shortcomings are fewer in number than those of anyone else. Moreover, Blaise is immediately aware of them himself, so that he becomes eager to change. Self-correction is, in fact, one of the musts of the cure; although the islanders explain to the Europeans that they may seek advice and understanding, the initative for change must originate in them and stem from an inward desire for proper, reasonable conduct. Blaise, once cured, provides for much of the comicality of the play by spurring on the others to accomplish the brain repair necessary for normal size. Some of the Europeans, once persuaded that their pettiness of body is a reflection of their pettiness of soul, although resisting at first, give in, regret, and promise more rational behavior, in exchange for which their stature is restored to normalcy. Such is the case of the Courtier, Frontignac, the Countess, and Spinette. Things do not go smoothly, however, with the rest: the Doctor refuses to recognize that he makes a living by killing his patients; the Poet and the Philosopher persist in defending with insults and fists the alleged superiority of their profession.

L'Ile de la raison includes, in addition, a romantic element that involves two of the islanders, the Courtier and Countess. In treating it, Marivaux introduces the original twist of having on his island the women court the men, a practice that is just as normal for the natives as its opposite is for the Europeans. But no matter who the holders of initiative are, the happy ending of the comedy is provided by appropriate marriages, although the dénouement is somewhat modified by the Doctor, Poet, and Philosopher, who remain beyond help and are eternally dwarfed.

Obviously, the episodes concerning the incurables should have reminded the spectators and critics of like episodes in a number of Molière plays, but especially in *Le Bourgeois gentilhomme*, *Les Femmes savantes*, and *Le Malade imaginaire*. It is surprising indeed that, to date, this has not been the case. The famous dispute between the dancing teacher, the music instructor, the fencing master, and the philosopher in *Le Bourgeois gentilhomme* must have been at the root of Act I, Scene 8 and Act III, Scene 4 of Marivaux's comedy. In *Le Bourgeois gentilhomme*, the quarrel is generated by the pride and unreasonableness of each participant.

> LE MAITRE A DANSER: Je lui soutiens que la danse est une science à laquelle on ne peut faire assez d'honneur.
>
> LE MAITRE DE MUSIQUE: Et moi, que la musique en est une que tous les siècles ont révérée.
>
> LE MAITRE D'ARMES: Et moi, je leur soutiens à tous deux que la science de tirer des armes est la plus belle et la plus nécessaire de toutes les sciences.
>
> LE MAITRE DE PHILOSPHIE: Et que sera donc la philosophie? Je vous trouve tous trois bien impertinents de parler devant moi avec cette arrogance, et de donner impudemment le nom de science à des choses que l'on ne doit pas même honorer du nom d'art . . .
>
> LE MAITRE D'ARMES: Allez, philosophe de chien.
>
> LE MAITRE DE MUSIQUE: Allez, belître de pédant.
>
> LE MAITRE A DANSER: Allez, cuistre fieffé. . . . *Le philosophe se jette sur eux, et tous trois le chargent de coups . . . Ils sortent en se battant.* (II, 4)

Likewise, in Marivaux's play, the Poet and Philosopher try to diminish the importance of each other's discipline.

LE PHILOSOPHE: . . . idée poétique que cela, Monsieur le poète, car vous m'avez
    dit que vous l'étiez.

LE POETE: Ma foi, Monsieur de la philosophie, car vous m'avez dit que vous
    l'aimiez, une idée de poète vaut bien une vision de philosophe. (I, 8)

Moreover later, as in *Le Bourgeois gentilhomme*, the argument continues and degenerates into insults.

LE PHILOSOPHE: Il s'agit de cet impertinent-là [the Poet] qui a l'audace de faire des
    vers où il me satirise.

LE POETE: . . . ce sont des idées qui viennent et qui sont plaisantes; il faut que
    cela sorte; cela se fait tout seul. Je n'ai que les écrire, et cela aurait diverti
    le Gouverneur; un peu à vos dépens, à la vérité: mais c'est ce qui en fait
    tout le sel; et à cause que j'ai mis quelque épithète un peu maligne contre
    le philosophe, cela l'a mis en colère. . . .

LE PHILOSOPHE: Poète insolent! (III, 4)

Les Femmes savantes must have contributed also to parts of
Marivaux's scenes. It will be recalled that, in Molière's play, there is a
celebrated quarrel between a poet, Trissotin, and a philosopher,
Vadius:

TRISSOTIN, *à Vadius:* Avez-vous vu un certain petit sonnet sur la fièvre que tient la
    princesse Uranie?

VADIUS: . . . son sonnet ne vaut rien.

TRISSOTIN: J'en suis l'auteur. . . . Allez, petit grimaud, barbouilleur de papier.

VADIUS: Allez, rimeur de balle, opprobre du métier. . . . Ma plume t'apprendra
    quel homme je puis être. (III, 5)

Of course, it is true that Molière might have borrowed the subject of
similar disputes from actual living situations: "Une scène sembiable à
celle de Trissotin et de Vadius avait eu lieu entre Ménage et Cotin, chez
Mademoiselle, fille de Gaston de France."[4] It is also true that "the
quarrel between Trissotin and Vadius may have been inspired partly by
the *Comédie des académistes*."[5] Although such sources are plausible for
Molière, they become less probable in the case of Marivaux, who, in
view of the frequent inspiration he draws from his predecessor, could
not be said to have gone any further for his scenes than to Molière's
theater. Although the verbal similarites between *Le Bourgeois gentilhomme*, *Les Femmes savantes*, and *L'Ile de la raison* are few in
number, the quarrels between Molière's characters were so famous in
the early eighteenth century, so quoted, and so paraphrased, that
Marivaux surely wanted to capitalize on them.

Fragments of *Le Malade imaginaire* also may be noted in one of

[4]Molière, *Oeuvres* (Paris: G. Charpentier, n.d.), 552.
[5]Lancaster, *French Dramatic Literature*, 2, 738.

Marivaux's episodes. In the prologue of Molière's play, doctors are apostrophized as follows:

> Votre plus haut savoir n'est que pure chimère,
> Vains et peu sages médecins;
> Vous ne pouvez guérir . . .
> Ignorants médecins . . .

And later in the comedy Béralde attempts to demonstrate the futility of trusting doctors: "C'est de la meilleure foi du monde qu'il vous expédiéra; et il ne fera, en vous tuant, que ce qu'il a fait à sa femme et à ses enfants, et ce qu'en un besoin il ferait à lui-même" (III, 3). Similarly, the doctor in Marivaux's play not only is accused, but actually admits the guilt imputed by Béralde in Molière's version.

> BLAISE: Dites-moi, sans vous fâcher, étiez-vous en ménage, aviez-vous femme?
>
> LE MEDECIN: Non, je suis veuf; ma femme est morte à vingt-cinq ans d'une fluxion de poitrine.
>
> BLAISE: Maugré la doctraine de la Faculté?
>
> LE MEDECIN: Il ne me fut pas possible de la réchapper.
>
> BLAISE: Avez-vous des enfants?
>
> LE MEDECIN: Non.
>
> BLAISE: Ni en bian ni en mal?
>
> LE MEDECIN: Non, vous dis-je. J'en avais trois; et ils sont morts de la petite vérole, il y a quatre ans.
>
> BLAISE: Peste soit du docteur! et de quoi guarissiez-vous donc le monde? (II, 2)

Thus, both Molière's and Marivaux's doctors have failed to cure wife and children; Molière's doctors are *vains et peu sages*; Marivaux's is *sot*; finally, Molière's doctors are apostrophized with: *Vous ne pouvez guérir;* Marivaux's is asked with sarcasm: *et de quoi guarissiez-vous donc le monde?* However, as in the case of the previously mentioned similarities, it should be pointed out that Béralde's description again may be based on a living situation. Aimé Martin, for example, asserts: "Molière désigne peut-être ici le médecin Guénaut . . . qui, d'après le témoignage de Guy-Patin, avait tué, avec son remède favori (l'antimoine), sa femme, sa fille, son neveu et deux de ses gendres."[6] Although it is true that Molière was not the only comedy writer to satirize medicine,[7] and that irony against doctors was commonplace at the time, Molière is associated most closely with this type of sarcasm. Moreover, there are no definite similarities between Marivaux's irony against medicine and the irony of Boursault or of Hauteroche; whereas

[6]In Molière, *Oeuvres*, 660.
[7]Boursault wrote *Le Médecin volant* in 1664; Hauteroche composed *Crispin médecin* in 1670; and so forth.

the similarities pointed out between *Le Malade imaginaire* and *L'Ile de la raison* are rather specific.

It is interesting to note that in addition to the sources of inspiration Marivaux found in Molière, there are other instances of influence that may be traced to authors of the seventeenth century. For example, Marivaux's line "Non, des vers ne sont pas une marchandise" (I, 10) probably was suggested to the playwright by: "Je ne puis souffrir ces auteurs . . . qui . . . mettent leur Apollon aux gages d'un libraire, / et font d'un art divin un métier mercéniare" of Boileau's *Art poétique*. M. Duviquet, in his edition of the works of Marivaux, estimates that Act III, Scene 3, is a copy in miniature of La Bruyère's similar and frequent descriptions of the Court.[8] However, a reading of La Bruyère's texts does not reveal any specific similarities, and Duviquet admits that Marivaux's description is more daring than those of his predecessor.

It should be pointed out also that, for all its failure, *L'Ile de la raison* anticipates a number of important, indeed striking ideas propagated later on by other thinkers. An example is the following piece of dialogue between an islander, Blectrue, who has not heard of the word "poet," and the Poet.

LE POETE: On appelle cela des tragédies, que l'on récite en dialogues, où il y a des héros si tendres, qui ont tour à tour des transports de vertu et de passion si merveilleux; de nobles coupables qui ont une fierté si étonnante, dont les crimes ont quelque chose de si grand, et les reproches qu'ils s'en font sont si magnanimes; des hommes enfin qui ont de si respectables faiblesses, qui se tuent quelquefois d'une manière si admirable et si auguste, qu'on ne saurait les voir sans en avoir l'âme émue et pleurer de plaisir. Vous ne me répondez rien.

BLECTRUE, *surpris, l'examine sérieusement:* Voilà qui est fini, je n'espère plus rien; votre espèce me devient plus problématique que jamais. Quel pot-pourri de crimes admirables, de vertus coupables et de faiblesses augustes! il faut que leur raison ne soit qu'un coq-à-l'âne. Continuez.

LE POETE: Et puis, il y a des comédies où je représentais les vices et les ridicules des hommes.

BLECTRUE: Ah! je leur pardonne de pleurer là.

LE POETE: Point du tout; cela les faisait rire.

BLECTRUE: Hem?

LE POETE: Je vous dis qu'ils riaient.

BLECTRUE: Pleurer où l'on doit rire, et rire où l'on doit pleurer! les monstrueuses créatures! (I, 10)

The preceding contains most of the ideas that Jean-Jacques Rousseau would expound some thirty years later in his celebrated *Letrtre à*

---

[8]In Marivaux's *Oeuvres complètes* (Paris: Haut-Coeur et Gayet Jeune, 1825-1830), 1, 314.

D'Alembert. Another instance of the anticipatory powers of Marivaux may be seen in the explanation the Governor of the Island offers with regard to the lack of religious ceremony in connection with marriage: "Quand on a de la raison, toutes les conventions sont faites" (III, 9). Paul Gazagne interpreted this speech as a plea on the part of the author for free love.[9] Be that as it may, such was the theory of anarchism as outlined a century later in France by Bukinin, and such are also, in part, the explanations offered today by those who favor no contracts between consenting adults. In fact, the Governor's speeches are all replete with ideas of an enlightened despot at a time when absolute monarchy was still the established regime. Of course, the very basis of the plot, challenging not only the prejudice of associating rationality with class but also the traditional role of the sexes in so far as love is concerned, gives to *L'Ile de la raison* aspects that make of it "moins une pièce qu'une dissertation philosophique."[10] Were it not for the *moliéresque* details cited, the social and philosophical preoccupations of the play would tend to detract from the pure humor one expects in a comedy. But, like Molière, who was so often able to weave serious problems into the very fabric of farce (in spite of his frequent assertation that all he wanted to do was *de faire rire*), Marivaux, by recalling standard *moliéresque* episodes, is equally able to combine laughter-causing and thought-provoking themes into a play that, through its success in the twentieth century, reaffirms the moderness of the playwright.

[9]Gazagne, *Marivaux par lui-même*, 101.
[10]Fleury, *Marivaux et le marivaudage*, 86.

LA (SECONDE) SURPRISE DE L'AMOUR

To date, no Marivaux specialist has pointed out resemblances between *La (Seconde) Surprise de l'amour* and Molière's comedies. Some critics have noticed similarities between the first *Surprise de l'amour* and certain scenes in Molière's theater,[1] and because the second *Surprise de l'amour* evolves around the same basic theme (two lovers who feign indifference towards each other before marriage), Molière's contribution to this theme should be brought into the picture too. Only E. J. H. Greene came close to suggesting a *moliéresque* influence when he called one of the characters of the play, Hortensius, a *moliéresque* personage; yet in the very same paragraph he stated, for unexplained reasons, that "it is idle to look elsewhere [other than in the first *Surprise de l'amour*] for sources."[2] On the contrary, two critics of Molière have noted, but without any specification, resemblances between *La Princesse d'Elide* and Marivaux's comedy. Maurice Donnay declared: "L'on voit que, par sa colère, son dépit, sa pudeur, sa curiosité . . . la princesse d'Elide deviendra la marquise de *La (Seconde) Surprise de l'amour*."[3] Georges Lafenestre made an even more sweeping statement when he wrote: "Marivaux, au théâtre, cherche son inspiration dans les oeuvres oubliées qu'on ne lit guère. . . . *La Princesse d'Elide* lui fournit des scènes assez nombreuses dans *Les Surprises de l'amour*."[4]

To begin with, *La (Seconde) Surprise de l'amour* shares with *La Surprise de l'amour* only the basic plot. In both comedies there is a pair of lovers who conceal their sentiments from each other before marriage. Beyond this similarity, the details are quite different. In the play under discussion, the Marquise, a widow faithful to the memory of her husband, has decided to spend the rest of her life in seclusion mourning his death. The Chevalier, a neighbor, has lost his girlfriend to religion; Angélique has become a nun rather than marry the man proposed by her father. As in the previous *Surprise*, the two misanthropists are attracted to each other, but whereas in the first play there was the additional pretense of lack of friendship, in this one, the Marquise and the Chevalier delude themselves with the thought that amity will be sufficient and need not deteriorate into love. The relationship that ensues is one of respect for each other's hurt. Little do they suspect that those who hurt together begin to hurt less and, as the suffering di-

[1]See chapter on the first *Surprise de l'amour*.
[2]Greene, *Marivaux*, 112.
[3]Donnay, *Molière*, 309.
[4]Georges Lafenestre, *Molière* (Paris: Hachette, 1909), 192-193.

minishes, they are once more *disponsible*. Such disponsibility is helped by the machinations of the Marquise's servant, Lisette, and the valet of the Chevalier, Lubin. In addition, a catalyst appears, the Count. He it is, who, aspiring to marry the Marquise, provokes the jealousy of the Chevalier, and thus crystallizes the love that he had mistaken previously for mere friendship. Similarly falsely informed by Hortensius that the Chevalier does not want to marry her and has indeed spurned her, the Marquise's *amour-propre* is piqued to the point where she no longer confuses love with friendship either. Thus, misunderstanding and *dépit amoureux* provide for a mutual unmasking of the lover's sentiments, and once more two persons who have resisted love, yet have continued to play the game, find themselves entrapped and seeming indifference results in marriage.

Kenneth N. McKee plays down the comparison between *La (Seconde) Surprise de l'amour* and *La Surprise de l'amour*. He writes: "Marivaux had made much progress in his ability to delineate awakening love during the five-year period between the two plays. One senses a more polished mastery of thought and style."[5] In fact, scorn for the other sex, which was the common ground that separated the Countess and Lélio of *La Première surprise*, less believable, is absent from *La (Seconde) Surprise de l'amour*, in which the motive for separation, personal grief, becomes at the same time, though gradually, the bond that will unite the two neighbors. Moreover, the sententious preachings on love and infidelity that one finds in the first *surprise* are absent from the second, which is free from moralizing and freer of what antagonists of Marivaux call *marivaudage*. An example of such improvement can be seen in one of the speeches of the Marquise, which is full of penetration, self-analysis, and skill, one which a less experienced playwright could not have written, "Je ne veux point me marier, mais je ne veux pas qu'on me refuse" (II, 4). And a little later she explains her reasoning.

> LA MARQUISE: Eh! Monsieur, mon veuvage est éternel; en vérité, il n'y a point de femme au monde plus éloignée du mariage que moi, et j'ai perdu le seul homme qui pouvait me plaire; mais malgré tout cela, il y a de certaines aventures désagréables pour une femme. Le Chevalier m'a refusée, par exemple; mon amour-propre ne lui en veut aucun mal; il n'y a là-dedans, comme je vous l'ai déjà dit, que le ton, que la manière que je condamne: car, quand il m'aimerait, cela lui serait inutile; mais enfin il m'a refusée, cela est constant, il peut se vanter de cela, il le fera peut-être; qu'en arrive-t-il? Cela jette un air de rebut sur une femme, les égards et l'attention qu'on a pour elle en diminuent, cela glace tous les esprits pour elle; je ne parle point des coeurs, car je n'en ai que faire: mais on a besoin

de considération dans la vie, elle dépend de l'opinion qu'on prend de
vous; c'est l'opinion qui nous donne tout, qui nous ôte tout, au point
qu'après tout ce qui m'arrive, si je voulais me remarier, je le suppose, à
peine m'estimerait-on quelque chose, il ne serait plus flatteur de m'aimer;
le Comte, s'il savait ce qui s'est passé, oui, le Comte, je suis persuadée
qu'il ne voudrait plus de moi. (II, 6)

It would seem, then, that Marivaux specialists notwithstanding, the
source of the second *surprise* cannot be said to be the first alone. And
even if that were the case, because *La Première surprise de l'amour* has
been shown to have a number of *moliéresque* sources, it stands to reason
that the second does also, as indeed the two Molière critics quoted
above have indicated. A close perusal of Marivaux's text uncovers
those passages in Molière's plays that he probably had in mind when he
wrote his comedy. These passages are to be found in *La Princesse
d'Elide, Le Bourgeois gentilhomme,* and *Les Femmes savantes.*

Molière's Princesse d'Elide and the Marquise share a desire not to
get married. Their reasons are different, to be sure (the Princess
because she naturally despises men; the Marquise because she wants
to remain faithful to the memory of her first husband), but they both
feign a desire for solitude, an indifference toward the opposite sex. This
results in a number of similar scenes. In Molière's play, the Princess,
hearing that Eurayle does not wish to win her heart, declares to her
cousin: "Ne trouvez-vous pas qu'il y aurait d'abaisser son orgueil, et de
soumettre un peu ce coeur qui tranche tant du brave? . . . Je vous
avoue que cela m'a donné de l'émotion, et que je souhaiterais fort de
trouver les moyens de châtier cette hauteur . . . et employer toute
chose pour lui donner de l'amour" (II, 5). Similarly, in Marivaux's play,
the Marquise, having learned that the Chevalier is not interested in
marrying her, exclaims with indignation: "Se récrier devant les domes-
tiques, m'exposer à leur raillerie, ah! c'en est un peu trop; il n'y a point
de situation qui dispense d'être honnête. . . . Oh! je vous assure que
je mettrais ordre à cela. Comment donc! cela m'attaque directement,
cela va presque au mépris. Oh! Monsieur le Chevalier, aimez votre
Angélique tant que vous voudrez; mais que je n'en souffre pas, s'il vous
plaît!" (II, 4). Both girls are indignant because of a similar action on the
part of a man, and the *je mettrais ordre à cela* of the Marquise expresses
the same plan as is expressed in the *je souhaiterais . . . employer toute
chose pour lui donner de l'amour* of the Princess.

In another instance, the Princess, not being able to overcome and
eliminate the apparent indifference of Eurayle, admits to herself: "Cet
orgueil me confond, et j'ai un tel dépit que je ne me sens pas" (III, 4).
Likewise, the Marquise expresses her own self-pity: "Je suis rejetée,
j'essuie des affronts . . . qu'une femme est à plaindre dans la situation

où je suis! . . . Et comment me traite-t-on! . . . Le Chevalier m'a refusée. . . . Me voilà déroutée, je ne sais plus comment régler ma conduite . . . j'ai besoin, pour réparation, que son discours [that of the Chevalier refusing to marry her] n'ait été qu'un dépit amoureux" (II, 6). The Marquise's *je ne sais plus comment régler ma conduite* reflects the *je ne me sens pas* of the Princess. And, of course, Euryale's rejection of the Princess is due to a *dépit amoureux,* and so is the Chevalier's refusal to marry the Marquise.

An even more striking resemblance may be revealed. Having heard that Euryale is interested in another girl, the Princess complains to Moron, valet of the Court, of her unendurable destiny; whereupon the following dialogue takes place:

> MORON: Mais, madame, s'il vous aimait, vous n'en voudriez point, et cependant vous ne voulez pas qu'il soit à une autre . . .
>
> LA PRINCESSE: Non, je ne puis souffrir, qu'il soit heureux avec une autre; et, si la chose était, je crois que j'en mourrais de déplaisir.
>
> MORON: Ma foi, madame, avouez la dette. Vous voudriez qu'il fût à vous. (III, 6)

In Marivaux's play, a similar situation and dialogue occur: the Marquise, having found out that the Chevalier will marry the Count's sister, cries on the shoulder of her maid: "Le Chevalier est sorti, il se marie aussi; le Comte lui donne sa soeur; car il ne me manquait qu'une soeur, pour achever de me déplaire, à cet homme-là" (III, 12). Whereupon Lisette echoes Moron's arguments; "Quand le Chevalier l'épouserait, que vous importe?" (III, 12). And the Marquise's answer, less eloquent and more subtle than that of the Princess, nevertheless expresses the latter's feelings to the letter: "Veux-tu que je sois la belle-soeur d'un homme qui m'est devenu insupportable?" (III, 12). Thus, Marivaux's dialogue differs little from that of Molière. Likewise, both the Princess and the Marquise share identical sentiments; they both show their despair to a servant, and both servants react in similar manner. Maurice Donnay and Georges Lafenestre, then, although failing to be specific, appear to have been correct in their statements concerning the influence of Molière on *La (Seconde) Surprise de l'amour*.

The actions and the vocabulary of Hortensuis in Marivaux's comedy probably were inspired by the well-known words and deeds of the teacher of philosophy in Molière's *Le Bourgeois gentilhomme*. Both characters claim to have a great amount of admiration for the ancients, for the powers and utility of reason. Moreover, they are both pedants and they both fill and act an analogously comic role. The reliance of the teacher of philosophy on Seneca. "N'avez-vous pas lu le docte traité que Sénèque a composé de la colère? . . . et la raison ne doit-elle pas être maîtresse de tous nos mouvements?" (II, 4), is emulated by

Hortensius, who also praises reason and Seneca: "La raison est d'un prix à qui tout cède; c'est elle qui fait notre véritable grandeur; on a nécessairement toutes les vertus avec elle; enfin le plus respectable de tous les hommes, ce n'est pas le plus puissant, c'est le plus raisonnable" (II, 8). And when the Chevalier contradicts Hortensius and calls him *un petite auteur*, the latter becomes indignant: "Petit auteur. . . . Un homme qui cite Sénèque pour garant de ce qu'il dit . . ." (II, 8). Later in the same scene, like the teacher of philosophy who had lost his temper in Molière's play despite Seneca, Hortensius also became angry and stormed out of the room, swearing, "Sénèque un petit auteur! Par Jupiter" (II, 8).

Another source for *La (Seconde) Surprise de l'amour* was probably *Les Femmes savantes*. It will be recalled that Bélise and Philaminte are angry at their servant, Martine, because she cannot appreciate the value of science, of books, of art. When she is about to be dismissed, Martine revolts. "Tout ce que vous prêchez est, je crois, bel et bon, / Mais je ne saurais, moi, parler votre jargon. . . . / Mon Dieu! je n'avons pas étugué comme vous" (II, 6). Lubin, in Marivaux's play, also displays ignorance and scorns education, books, and science: "*Chargé d'une manne de livres, et s'asseyant dessus:* Ah! je n'aurais jamais cru que la science fût si peasante" (II, 1). Moreover, Lisette likewise makes fun of Hortensius. "A mon égard, je salue votre érudition, et je suis votre très humble servante" (III, 2). Only the vocabulary used is different; the situations are alike; that is, both plays show the aversion of servants to the pedantry of the masters or of persons employed by the masters. To be sure, this type of servant is not uncommon in the dramatic literature of the seventeenth and eighteenth centuries; nevertheless the similarities are worth observing in this context. It is also noteworthy that Bélise and Philaminte have hired Trissotin to further their education, just as the Marquise hired Hortensius to read for her and to give her lessons. Kenneth N. McKee's assertion that Hortensius' "ancestry might be traced back to Sorel's *Francion* or to comic types in the old Italian repertory"[6] is in keeping with the critic's preference for attributing remote sources to Marivaux's plays rather than acknowledging the clear and more tenable *moliéresque* influences. An attentive perusal of *Francion* proves entirely unrewarding insofar as pinpointing with any measure of exactitude Marivaux's reliance on it; of course, it is equally difficult, if not more so, to discover possible sources of influence in the largely unavailable old Italian repertory. On the other hand, Hortensius represents the often-met *moliéresque* teacher-writer who is unsuccessful

⁶*Ibid.*, 102.

but nevertheless is capable of earning a living through the admiration of feminine audiences (at times the audience may be masculine, as in the case of Monsieur Jourdain) attempting to acquire more *esprit*.

It should be pointed out, also, that the topic of a widow faithful to the memory of her deceased husband but awakening to love when a *premier venu* appears had been dealt with by Petronius in his *Matrone d'Ephèse*. The theme of a woman who cannot resist the courtship of an engaging man despite the recent loss of her husband had been treated also by a close friend of Marivaux, Houdar de la Motte, in his own *Matrone d'Ephèse* (1702). Earlier versions of the subject, Mainfray's *L'Ephèsienne* (1614) and Fatouville's *La Matrone d'Ephèse* (1681), bear no specific similarities with Marivaux's comedy, nor do any of the other titles mentioned herein. This is corroborated by Jean Fleury[7] and Kenneth N. McKee,[8] both of whom refer to the earlier versions of the subject without hinting at the possibility of imitation. Gustave Larroumet's assertion that "Regnard pourrait réclamer comme sienne l'invention de la scène VIII, acte II, de la seconde *Surprise de l'Amour*,"[9] is debatable; although Regnard has one of his characters quote from Seneca in Act IV, Scene 13, the ancient's comments on money are cited, not his opinions on the power of reason, which interest Hortensius. Be that as it may, only the *moliéresque* recollections are specific enough and persistent enough to warrant indication.

These recollections, unperceived by Marivaux's contemporaries just as they were ignored in the case of other plays previously mentioned, failed to contribute to success at the Théâtre Français. Yet, *La (Seconde) Surprise de l'amour* was among the playwright's favorites.[10] Marivaux must have sensed that, in the words of the critic for the *Mercure de France*, "Toutes les voix se réunissent à dire que la dernière *Surprise de l'Amour*, est une pièce parfaitement bien écrite, pleine d'esprit & de sentimens; que c'est une métaphysique de coeur très-délicate. . . . Le sujet est trop simple, dit-on, soit; mais c'est de cette même simplicité que l'Auteur doit tirer une nouvelle gloire."[11] A more recent reviewer, Arthur Tilley, confirmed: "The skillful fashion in which Marivaux deals with the effect of . . . cross-currents upon . . . feelings is a part of the mastery of his art to which he had now attained."[12] Notwithstanding the fact that *La (Seconde) Surprise de*

[7]Fleury, *Marivaux et le marivaudage*, 124.

[8]McKee, *Theater of Marivaux*, 103.

[9]Larroumet, *Marivaux, sa vie et ses oeuvres*, 156.

[10]Together with *La Première Surprise de l'amour, La Double inconstance, La Mère confidente, Les Serments indiscrets, Les Sincères*, and *L'Epreuve*.

[11]*Le Mercure de France* (Paris), December 1727, pp. 2957-2958.

[12]Tilley, *Three French Dramatists*, 120.

l'amour is a masterpiece of analysis, especially in its totality, in its atmosphere in which internal obstacles dominate external ones, the cool reception accorded to it can be explained, probably, once again in terms of the inability of the playwright's contemporaries to recognize some of its *moliéresque* aspects quoted above. In this connection, one of the comments of the critic for the *Mercure de France* is especially noteworthy: "Le genre que Molière a consacré au Théâtre François est le seul qu'on y cherche."[13]

Marivaux's originality in the play, especially in his delineation of the Marquise's sexuality that makes her different from the more youthful and less coquettish Princesse d'Elide, might have contributed also to the lack of success of his comedy. It will be recalled that the stage indications specify that the Marquise must appear in a *négligée*, a garment that Marivaux had defined previously as "un honnête équivalent de la nudité même."[14] Far from Cornelian, the Marquise's constant concern bears on how she appears to people, on how able she is to conquer, to flirt, on how she might assert all the feminine charms at her disposal; this, without regard for contradiction, in a deluge of words where the true and the false coexist matter-of-factly. The result must have been a bit confusing for the classically tuned audience of the Théâtre Français, and would have gone over much better at the Théâtre Italien. In fact, *La (Seconde) Surprise de l'amour* was presented by Roger Planchon, in his now famous 1959 production, in a Brechtian light, as well he should have done for twentieth-century spectators: capitalizing on the Marquise's frivolity, he placed her and the Count into bed together, at the end of Scene 9. Here indeed was sensuality Marivaux perhaps never had dreamt about. Yet, if such an interpretation had occurred in the mind of an eighteenth-century spectator, surely the acceptability of the comedy would have been diminished greatly. The modernity of the Marquise in those of her characteristics that make her differ from the more familiar aspects of the Princesse d'Elide must have reduced, then, Marivaux's chances of acceptance. For present-day viewers, however, *La (Seconde) Surprise de l'amour* pleases and interests both because it treats *moliéresque* themes and because of its originality.

---

[13]*Le Mercure de France* (Paris), December 1727, p. 2957.
[14]Marivaux, *Oeuvres complètes* (Paris: Editions Duchesne, 1881), 9, 400.

LE TRIOMPHE DE PLUTUS

Following his moderate failure at the Théâtre Français, Marivaux returned after a two-year absence to the Théâtre Italien with the one act of *Le Triomphe de Plutus*. Perhaps because of the rather unimportant part this comedy plays in the development of the playwright's theatrical endeavors, it is rarely presented and it is infrequently mentioned in critical works. At any rate, neither Marivaux specialists nor critics of Molière have associated it with the equally ignored and seldom staged *La Comtesse d'Escarbagnas* of the seventeenth-century playwright.

The plot of *Le Triomphe de Plutus* deals with the rivalry of Apollo and Plutus for the love of Aminte. Following a bet, the two gods descend to earth, Plutus under the guise of a financier, Richard, and Apollo wearing the mask of a writer, Ergaste. His beauty and his intelligence notwithstanding, Apollo finds it difficult to provide Plutus with a real fight. The latter, whose aim is to prove that in love, as in anything else, money is all powerful, succeeds in winning her heart by means of liberalities extended to the servants of Aminte and to Aminte herself. While Apollo wastes his time attempting to conquer with well-conceived rhymes, Plutus distributes money and presents to Spinette, Aminte's chambermaid, to Amidas, the uncle, in fact to everyone in sight. At the end of the play, Apollo undertakes to compose a *divertissement* for his financée, while Plutus counters with: "Ergaste vous fait là-haut des vers; chacun a sa poésie, et voilà la mienne" (Scene 10); and he hands her an expensive bracelet. Overcome by such lavishness, Spinette, who speaks for her mistress, concludes: "Une rime à ces vers-là serait bien riche"; and "Il y a dans ses manières je ne sais quoi d'engageant qui vous entraîne" (Scene 10). Thus, the end of the play departs from the convention that requires that vice be punished and goodness rewarded. Apollo remarks sadly, "Il ne manquait plus que ce trait pour achever ma défaite; et me voilà pleinement convaincu que l'argent est l'unique divinité à qui les hommes sacrifient" (Scene 17). The *dénouement* is somewhat modified, however, when the two gods reveal their identity and depart, telling the assembly to enjoy the festivities already paid for, as well as the bounty left behind.

Although the theme of *La Comtesse d'Escarbagnas* is somewhat different, it will be recalled that Monsieur Harpin, one of the suitors of the Countess, pays her household expenses in return for promises of fidelity, which, apparently, are not kept. Monsieur Harpin, on whom perhaps the character of Plutus was modeled, discovers, like his eighteenth-century counterpart, that one of his rivals is preparing a *divertissement,* and he decides to disrupt it by using uncivil language

62

and threats. The Countess accuses Monsieur Harpin: "Mais, vraiment, on ne vient point ainsi se jeter au travers d'une comédie, et troubler un acteur qui parle" (Scene 21). And Monsieur Harpin replies: "Hé! têtebleu! la véritable comédie qui se fait ici" (Scene 21), after which he goes on to express his scorn in no uncertain terms. In Marivaux's play, when the audience manifests its indifference to the *divertissement* given by Apollo, Plutus, who is more polite than Monsieur Harpin but no less efficacious in his aims, declares simply, "C'est que les musiciens ont la voix enrouée; il faut un peu graisser ces gosiers-là" (Scene 12).

In addition, Monsieur Harpin and Plutus annoy part of their audience with their manner of speaking, untrained as they are in the civilities of the *gens de qualité*. Such expressions as *têtebleu* are followed by Monsieur Harpin with *morbleu, ventrebleu, quittons la faribole, etc.* The Countess shows her revulsion to these manners by objecting, "Hé! fi, monsieur! que cela est vilain de jurer de la sorte! . . . Je suis confuse de cette insolence" (Scene 21). Likewise in Marivaux's comedy, Apollo advises Plutus to change his manner of speaking: "Ecoutez, Seigneur Plutus; si elle a l'esprit délicat, je ne vous conseille pas de vous servir avec elle d'expressions si massives . . . ce style de douairière la rebuterait" (Scene 2).

To summarize, both Monsieur Harpin and Plutus are financiers (although the latter in disguise only); they are both vulgar in their approach; they both have to fight against a rival *de bel esprit;* the two lack manners and practice insolence; finally, they both disrupt and mock the *divertissement* put on by their rivals.[1]

Of course, the resemblances between *La Comtesse d'Escarbagnas* and *Le Triomphe de Plutus* are not so extensive as in the case of plays previously discussed. It may be that Marivaux was thinking more of Lesage's *Turcaret* when he wrote his comedy, but even if this is so, one ought to keep in mind Charles Louandres' commentary in his edition of Molière's works. According to his view, Monsieur Harpin, "Dans lequel l'insolence, la galanterie grossière des traitants sont pour la première fois mises en scène, semble avoir inspiré à Lesage l'idée de *Turcaret*."[2] Kenneth N. McKee,[3] Gustave Larroumet[4] and E. J. H. Greene[5] have noted the possible influence of *Turcaret* but without specifying the exact instances of similarity. The resemblances between

[1]For a detailed study of the role of financiers in French comedy, see J. Forkey, *The Rôle of Money in French Comedy* (Baltimore: Johns Hopkins University Press, 1956).
[2]See Charles Louandres' remarks in Molière, *Oeuvres* (Paris: Charles Louandres, 1885), 3, 478.
[3]McKee, *Theater of Marivaux*, 111-112.
[4]Larroumet, *Marivaux, sa vie et ses oeuvres*, 156.
[5]Greene, *Marivaux*, 116.

the two comedies are as follows: I, 4, of *Turcaret* and Scene 10 of *Le Triomphe de Plutus* (both financiers, Plutus and Turcaret, offering jewels to the woman they love); I, 6, of *Turcaret* and Scenes 4 and 5 of *Le Triomphe de Plutus* (Turcaret and Plutus bribing the servants); II, 3, of *Turcaret* and Scene 1 of Marivaux's play (both Plutus and Turcaret using vulgar language). In addition, Plutus and Turcaret share basic traits of character that result often in similar actions and reactions: use of uncivil vocabulary, tendency to buy people and sentiments, lack of appreciation for the finer things of life, and, in general, a display of poor upbringing. One difference between the two should be pointed out also: Turcaret deludes himself in his bestowal of gifts on others, for they buy him only infidelities, whereas Plutus manages in fact to acquire, through money, that which he wishes to purchase. Moreover, the aim of Marivaux was probably different from that of Lesage and closer to that of Molière. Whereas Lesage attempted to arouse indignation against tax collectors in order to complement, on a literary level, the witchhunt against the Government's corrupt fiscal representatives, a witchhunt that was taking place in the first decade of the eighteenth century; and whereas by 1728, when Marivaux presented his play, the public's outcry had long subsided, the country enjoyed a period of peace and prosperity, and financiers were accepted more than under the highly authoritarian regime of Louis XIV. Gustave Larroumet confirms that, "cuirassés par l'habitude, les financiers avaient pris leur parti des attaques dont ils pouvaient être l'objet; elles ne troublaient pas plus leur orgueil que leur quiétude. . . . Ici, il [Marivaux] se contente de railler agréablement les vices que Lesage a flétris: insolence et lourdeur, ignorance et grossièreté, prétentions risibles, ostentation de prodigalité, surtout en amour. A peine, en deux ou trois passages, une saillie mordante, et encore est-ce plutôt le sourire discret de l'homme d'esprit qui se venge des sots que le rire indigné du satirique."[6] *Le Triomphe de Plutus*, then, like *La Comtesse d'Escarbagnas*, does not have any social pretentions because it does not seek changes or ameliorations of the status quo, things that Lesage rightly considered appropriate for his own time. Marivaux's comedy is written in a flippant tone, and E. J. H. Greene is correct to consider it merely a *revue:* "a skit, with song and dance, in which everything is exaggerated to the point of caricature. As in many present-day *revues* the underlying pessimism, the blasé attitude, is disguised by the speed of the developments and the brio of the action. The 'morality' is of the type found on the pages of the *Chansonniers:* a sweeping generalization in which

[6]Larroumet, *Marivaux, sa vie et ses oeuvres*, 242-243.

there is some truth."[7] Although one may agree with Jean Fleury's remarks that "Ce petit acte est la mise en scène, sous forme allégorique, de l'éternelle querelle entre l'esprit et l'argent, le savoir et la richesse,"[8] it did not pretend to mount an attack of any consequence against the prevailing role of money in society. Plutus, unlike Turcaret and very much like Monsieur Harpin, does not worry anybody and does not harm anybody directly. On the contrary, through their lack of savoir-faire and the free extension of liberalities, the two provide so much comic relief that one is tempted to ignore the more serious problems that underlie their behavior and that of their company. Notwithstanding instances of similarity that may be found between *Le Triomphe de Plutus* and *Turcaret*, Plutus' predecessor is, much more directly, the *moliéresque* character of Monsieur Harpin.

[7]Greene, *Marivaux*, 116-117.
[8]Fleury, *Marivaux et le marivaudage*, 97.

LES SERMENTS INDISCRETS

Only Georges Lafenestre detected, but once again without specification, the influence of Molière's *La Princesse d'Elide* on *Les Serments indiscrets*.[1] Yet, even before Marivaux presented his comedy at the Comédie Française in 1732, the story had circulated that it was still another one of the *surprise* plays of the dramatist. It was immediately associated with *La Surprise de l'amour* and *La (Seconde) Surprise de l'amour*, the *moliéresque* sources of which have been discussed before.

Referring to like comedies in Marivaux's repertory, Voltaire, who had heard of *Les Serments indiscrets* before its presentation, anticipated the lack of depth of the new play when he wrote to his friend Formont: "Nous allons avoir cet été une comédie en prose du sieur de Marivaux, sous le titre *Les Serments indiscrets*. Vous croyez bien qu'il y aura beaucoup de métaphysique et peu de naturel; et que les cafés applaudiront, pendant que les honnêtes gens n'entendront rien."[2] Later, but still before the première of the play, he wrote again to Formont referring to the coming theatrical season and remarked, "Nous aurons aussi *Les Serments indiscrets*, de Marivaux, où j'espère que je n'entendrai rien."[3] The cabalistic accusations in which Voltaire took part bore not only on Marivaux's mania for restating the theme of *surprise*, but also on his audacity to devote five full acts to it. Whereas *La Princesse d'Elide* is a very short play, and *La Surprise de l'amour* and *La (Seconde) Surprise de l'amour* are in three acts only, the length of *Les Serments indiscrets* contributed greatly to the debacle of the author's newest try at the Comédie Française. The *Mercure de France* described the reception as "une des plus tumultueuses,"[4] and Mademoiselle de Bar, in a letter to Piron, confirmed, "On siffle depuis le commencement du second acte jusqu'à la troisième scène du cinquième."[5] Marivaux himself may have had second thoughts about his play (not as regards the length, for when it was suggested to him that he might abbreviate or make other changes, he refused in no uncertain terms), because at one point he wrote a letter to Quinault-Dufresne, one of the principal actors of the Comédie, in which he mentioned a desire to withdraw it.[6] Be that as it may, the play was not withdrawn, was not modified, and suffered the demise mentioned above. In the House of Molière, the metaphysics of the heart were not accepted readily even when they were replete with

[1]Lafenestre, *Molière*, 192-193.
[2]Voltaire, *Correspondence* (Genève: Institut et Musée Voltaire, 1953), 2, 303.
[3]*Ibid.*, 325.
[4]*Le Mercure de France* (Paris), June 1732, p. 1408.
[5]Marivaux, *Théâtre Complet*, Fournier and Bastide Edition, 2, 62.
[6]*Ibid.*, 36.

moliéresque reminiscences, noticed or not. In point of fact, it was natural that the audience of the Théâtre Français should prefer the conservative practitioners of the noble genres, that is, of tragedies and comedies written in accordance with seventeenth-century rules. Marivaux's writing, which had already a reputation of being somewhat artificial, committed, with *Les Serments indiscrets,* the additional error of lengthening the usual three-act format. On the occasion of a subsequent presentation, the signs of rejection subsided, and Piron wrote:

> Le calme succède à l'orage.
> Ce jour, poussé d'un heureux vent,
> Le parterre applaudit l'ouvrage
> Sifflé deux jours auparavant.

But he contends that the reader of the play will agree with the original detractors:

> Et poussé par un vent contraire,
> Sur le théâtre ayant à faux
> Applaudi monsieur Marivaux,
> Fut le siffler chez le libraire.[7]

Lesage himself, in his play *Les Désespérés,* wrote a line in which one of the characters expresses the hope that the Comédie Française will be spared in the future, "de Nouveaux serments."[8]

The topic of *Les Serments indiscrets* revolves around Lucile, whose father has chosen Damis as his future son-in-law. Both young people, however, have reservations about the forthcoming marriage, and both vow to do their best to prevent it. In the course of the first encounter, the *surprise* of mutual attraction occurs, yet face must be saved at all costs, or almost. The youthful error of making an imprudent vow is compounded in Lucile and Damis by the pride that prevents them from recanting. Lucile's father, Orgon, decides to offer Damis his younger daughter, Phénice, in order to make amends. Spitefully and without love, Damis accepts, and so does Lucile, who is goaded by the same *dépit amoureux*. Phénice alone sees clearly through the pretenses and the words expressing them, and realizes that beneath the temper and fickleness of the Damis-Lucile couple there is true love. Phénice uses her perspicacity to crush the lovers' spite, and eventually succeeds in having them confess their love for each other.

It is immediately evident that the thinness of the plot, already overextended in the three-act format of the dramatist's previous repertory hardly could hold the public's attention in a full-length play. Marivaux attempted to defend his audacity and the accusation of

[7] Alexis Piron, *Oeuvres* (Paris: Duchesne, 1885), 6, 322.
[8] Alain René Lesage, *Oeuvres choisies* (Paris: Veuve Pissot, 1737), 16, 182.

repetition by writing in the *Avertissement* that in the other *Surprises* the lovers "ignorent l'état de leur coeur, et sont le jouet du sentiment qu'ils ne soupçonnent point en eux; c'est là ce qui fait le plaisant du spectacle qu'ils donnent; les autres, au contraire, savent ce qui se passe en eux, mais ne voudraient ni le cacher, ni le dire, et assurément, je ne vois rien là dedans qui se ressemble." And then he went on to explain: "c'est qu'on y a vu le même genre de conversation et de style; c'est que ce sont des mouvements de coeur dans les deux pièces; et cela leur donne un air d'uniformité qui fait qu'on s'y trompe." However, the difference he mentions is not sufficient to eliminate the repetition, and the similarities he indicates, especially in view of the length of the play, are apt to provide for a certain measure of monotony. E. J. H. Greene confirms: "His assertions in the *Avertissement* about the originality of *Les Serments indiscrets* are quite accurate; but this time it was Marivaux himself who could not see the wood for the trees. For everyone else, the basic structure is that of the two *Surprises*. Two young people who, for one reason or another, have decided to remain single are brought together, and surprised by love."[9] But whatever the merits or demerits of *Les Serments indiscrets,* not only is a comparison with *La Princesse d'Elide* warranted by the presence of the latter play in the first two *Surprises,* but it is also helpful in defining Marivaux's dependence on his seventeenth-century predecessor.

The reasons of Moliere's Princess for not wanting to marry are echoed by Lucile in Marivaux's comedy. The former's comments: "Je ne veux point du tout me commettre à ces gens qui font les esclaves auprès de nous, pour devenir un jour nos tyrans. Toutes ces larmes, tous ces soupirs, tous ces hommages, tous ces respects, sont des embûches qu'on tend à notre coeur, et qui souvent l'engagent à commettre des lâchetés" (II, 1) are, in succinct form, those of the latter, who also scorns the tyranny of men:

Je les connais un peu, ces Messieurs-là; je remarque que les hommes ne sont bons qu'en qualité d'amants; c'est la plus jolie chose du monde que leur coeur, quand l'espérance les tient en haleine; soumis, respectueux et galants, pour le peu que vous soyez aimable avec eux, votre amour propre est enchanté; il est servi délicieusement; on le rassasie de plaisirs; folie, fierté, dédain, caprices, impertinences, tout nous réussit, tout est raison, tout est loi; on règne, on tyrannise, et nos idolâtres sont toujours à genoux. Mais les épousez-vous, la déesse s'humanise-t-elle, leur idolâtrie finit où nos bontés commencent. Dès qu'ils sont heureux, les ingrats ne méritent plus de l'être. (I, 2)

To be sure, the Princess' seventeenth-century concept of honor is not found in Lucile's speech. And, granted that Marivaux might merely express here what is an ancient and legendary complaint of women (that

[9]Greene, *Marivaux*, 146.

men are good to them only before marriage), it should be noted, nevertheless, that Lucile stresses in men as *amants* the same qualities that the Princess saw in them: *Toutes ces larmes, tous ces soupirs, tous ces hommages, tous ces respects,* of the Princess are echoed by Lucile's *soumis, respectueux et galants . . . tout nous réussit, tout est raison, tout est loi.* Moreover, the idea of men as *esclaves . . . pour devenir un jour nos tyrans* is translated by Lucile in *leur idolâtrie finit où nos bontés commencent.* It should be pointed out, also, that, whereas the Princess' and Lucile's comments might be similar only because they represent the standard thinking of women on the subject, both offer them as arguments against marriage.

Having vowed not to be the wife of the man she loves, the Princess, nevertheless, has the following request to make of Moron: "Parle-lui [to Euryale] de moi dans tes entretiens; vante-lui adroitement ma personne . . . et tâche d'ébranler ses sentiments par la douceur de quelque espoir. Je te permets de dire tout ce que tu voudras, pour tâcher à me l'engager . . . . Je souhaite ardemment qu'il m'aime" (III, 5). Similarly, Lucile orders her *suivante* to act on her behalf: "Je vous charge donc d'aller trouver Damis comme de vous-même, entendez-vous? . . . Il y a une certaine tournure, certaine industrie que vous pouvez employer: vous aurez remarqué mes discours, vous m'aurez vue inquiète, j'aurai soupiré si vous voulez . . . cependant persuadez Damis, dites-lui qu'il vienne, qu'il avoue hardiment qu'il m'aime; que vous sentez que je le souhaite" (IV, 9). It is evident, then, that Lucile's instructions echo those of the Princess: the latter attempts to conquer Euryale by means of *la douceur de quelque espoir,* the former with *discours . . . vue inquiète,* sighs, that are tantamount to a tacit declaration of love.

Molière's play seems to have influenced Marivaux's in another circumstance. Euryale, in order to awaken the *dépit amoureux* in the Princess, has shown an interest in Aglante, cousin of the latter. The marriage of Euryale and Aglante is soon in sight, and of course the Princess attempts to convince her cousin to renounce the project: "J'ai à vous prier d'une chose qu'il faut absolument que vous m'accordiez. Le prince d'Ithaque vous aime, et veut vous demander au prince mon père . . . mais je vous conjure de rejeter cette proposition, et de ne point prêter l'oreille à tout ce qu'il pourra vous dire" (IV, 3). Likewise, in Marivaux's comedy Damis has no choice but to show an interest in Phénice, and the marriage of Damis to Phénice is a semiaccepted event to come. Lucille, who of course loves Damis, tries to dissuade her sister from the projected marriage: "C'est que je vous persécuterai jusqu'à ce que vous ayez quitté cet amour-là; c'est que je ne veux point que vous le gardiez, et vous ne le garderez point; c'est moi qui vous le dis, qui vous en empêcherai bien. Aimer Damis! épouser Damis! Ah! je suis votre soeur, et il n'en sera rien" (IV, 7). Moreover, the reactions of Aglante and of Phénice are similar. Aglante questions, "Mais, madame, s'il était vrai que ce prince m'aimât effectivement, pourquoi n'ayant aucun dessein de vous engager, ne voudriez-vous pas souffrir? [that Euryale marry Aglante, speech interrupted by the Princess]" (IV, 3). Phénice, on her part, referring to the marriage Lucile wants her to renounce, objects in like fashion: "En vérité, vous m'étonnez; car je croyais que vous vous réjouiriez avec moi, parce que je vous débarrasse" (IV, 7).

La Princesse d'Elide probably provided the source for still other episodes in Marivaux's play. The following piece of dialogue from Molière's comedy:

> MORON: Ma foi, madame, avouons la dette. Vous voudriez qu'il [Euryale] fût à vous; et dans toutes vos actions, il est aisé de voir que vous aimez un peu ce jeune prince.
>
> LA PRINCESSE: Moi, je l'aime? O ciel! je l'aime? Avez-vous l'insolence de prononcer ces paroles? (III, 5)

appears to be at the root of the one in Marivaux's play quoted below:

> LISETTE: . . . enfin, il est temps de convenir que Damis ne vous déplaît point . . .
>
> LUCILE: Quand il vous plaira que je le haïsse, la recette est immanquable; vous n'avez qu'à me dire que je l'aime. (IV, 9)

Finally, one should note that, in both plays, the marriage of Euryale to Aglante and of Damis to Phénice, respectively, is only hours away. And in both plays, one final and successful attempt is made by the Princess and by Lucile to prevent the marriage in question. In each case, the plea is made to the father. In Molière's comedy the Princess begs:

> LA PRINCESSE, à Iphitas [her father]: Seigneur, je me jette à vos pieds pour vous demander une grâce . . . c'est de n'écouter point, seigneur, la demande de ce jeune prince, et de ne pas souffrir que la princesse Aglante soit unie avec lui.
>
> IPHITAS: Et par quelle raison, ma fille, voudrais-tu t'opposer à cette union?
>
> LA PRINCESSE: Par la raison que . . . il me devait aimer comme les autres, et me laisser au moins la gloire de le refuser . . . et ce m'est une honte sensible qu'à mes yeux, et au milieu de votre cour, il a recherché une autre que moi.
>
> IPHITAS: Et quelle offense te fait cela? tu ne veux accepter personne. (V, 2)

Marivaux's dialogue for the same situation is only slightly different. Lucile's arguments are all, in germ, those of the Princess.

> MONSIEUR ORGON: Ma fille, que signifie donc? . . . Comment! vous ne voulez pas voir le mariage de votre soeur? vous ne pardonnerez jamais? . . . et de quoi s'agit-il? de l'homme du monde qui vous est le plus indifférent!

LUCILE: . . . qu'on la marie au dépens du peu d'estime qu'on pouvait faire de mon esprit, de mon coeur, de mon caractère, je vous avoue, mon père, que cela est bien triste.

MONSIEUR ORGON: Mais que veux-tu dire? Tout ce que j'y vois, moi, c'est qu'elle est ta cadette, et qu'elle épouse un homme qui t'était destiné: mais ce n'est qu'à ton refus. Si tu avais voulu de Damis, il ne serait pas à elle, ainsi te voilà hors d'intérêt.

LUCILE: . . . mais je devais l'épouser . . . on ne revient jamais de l'accident humiliant qui m'arrive aujourd'hui . . . j'ai été dédaignée.

MONSIEUR ORGON: Tu es folle; on sait que tu as refusé Damis, encore une fois.
(V, 3)

Thus, Lucile's *j'ai été dédaignée,* which is her main argument, matches the *il m'a méprisée* previously quoted from V, 2, the principal argument of the Princess in the plea she makes of Iphitas. Moreover, from this point on, the ending of both comedies is similarly precipitous: Euryale confesses his scheme and declares his love for the Princess, and Phénice manages to have Damis throw himself at the feet of Lucile.

Yet, some details in *Les Serments indiscrets* are different. For example, in the beginning of Marivaux's play, both Damis and Lucile are against marriage, whereas in Molière's comedy only the Princess is against it, but Euryale is in favor of it. Another difference emerges from the character of Phénice, who is mature enough to understand the forces at play around her, and to bring the action to the happy ending she desires; whereas her counterpart in Molière's comedy, Aglante, is a pale and naïve creature with little or no bearing on the *dénouement*. These differences, however, do not obliterate the obvious recollections Marivaux used. Moreover, as has been pointed out already, although *La Princesse d'Elide* is modeled after Moreto's *El Desdén con el desdén,* there are no scenes or details in the Spanish play that bear a resemblance to *Les Serments indiscrets,* except for the main idea that, when two people are in love, feigned indifference on the part of one is bound to increase the intensity of love in the other; on the other hand, as has been shown, certain key scenes in *La Princesse d'Elide* have their counterpart in Marivaux's comedy.

Le Tartuffe, too, may have furnished the material for one of the scenes of *Les Serments indiscrets.* Gustave Larroumet noticed the similarity in a brief sentence, "La scène VII, acte III, des *Serments indiscrets,* entre Damis et Lucile, est une pâle copie de la fameuse scène du second acte de *Tartuffe* entre Marianne et Valère,"[10] but he did not compare the episodes in question. Molière's scene is, of course, well known: it deals with the quarrel between Valère and Marianne,

---

[10]Larroumet, *Marivaux, sa vie et ses oeuvres,* 193.

and with Dorine's attempts to reconcile the lovers. Part of the dialogue of this scene has been quoted already.[11] Marivaux uses once more the celebrated *moliéresque* theme for one of his own scenes in which the two youngsters engage in a spiteful dispute interrupted and finally settled by the servant, who displays more common sense than the masters:

> DAMIS: . . . *Il feint de s'en aller.*
>
> LUCILE: Qu'il s'en aille; l'arrêtera qui voudra.
>
> LISETTE: Eh! mais vous n'y pensez pas; revenez, donc, Monsieur; est-ce que la guerre est déclarée entre vous deux? . . . Mais quel est le travers qui vous prend à tous deux? Faut-il que des personnes qui se veulent du bien se parlent comme si elles ne pouvaient se souffrir? Et vous, Monsieur, qui aimez ma maitresse; car vous l'aimez, je gage. (III, 7)

Thus, Damis' wish to leave is but an echo of Valère's movements to the same effect; Lucile's *dépit* is a reflection of Marianne's sentiments because of which she makes no effort to stop Valère; and Lisette's intervention repeats that of Dorine almost to the letter (she stops Damis from leaving, just as Dorine stopped Valère; her *quel est le travers qui vous prend à tous deux* corresponds to Dorine's *Vous êtes fous tous deux;* and the assertion she makes that Damis loves Lucile repeats Dorine's *Il n'aime que vous seule, et n'a point d'autre envie que d'être votre époux; j'en réponds sur ma vie*).

Despite these similarities, Gustave Larroumet rightly speaks of Marivaux's version as a *pâle copie* of Molière's scene. The eighteenth-century playwright simply imitated the basic situation from *Le Tartuffe*, and some of the manifestations of spite of the two lovers (the man pretending to leave, and the girl failing to stop him), as well as some of the arguments of the servant, but he did not develop the comic possibilities of the scene by the swift dialogue that Molière used.

The relationship of *Les Serments indiscrets* to plays other than those of Molière is, at best, coincidental. Pierre Duviquet noted that Frontin's remark, "J'ai le caractère aussi vrai que la physionomie" (IV, 2) also is made by a servant, La Branche, in Lesage's *Crispin rival;* however, La Branche's affirmation is worded, "Je suis encore plus honnête que ma physionomie," and Duviquet admits that "Le mot de Frontin s'est trouvé sous la plume de Marivaux par suite d'une réminiscence involontaire."[12] Frédéric Deloffre observed that *Les Serments indiscrets* may have been suggested to Marivaux by Pierre Corneille's *Mélite*.[13] However, an attentive reading of *Mélite* does not indicate any imitation: Corneille's play simply deals with the common theme of feigned indif-

---

[11]See chapter on *Le Père prudent et équitable.*
[12]Pierre Duviquet, ed., *Oeuvres complètes de Marivaux* (Paris: Duviquet, 1830), 2, 94.
[13]Deloffre, *Marivaux et le marivaudage,* 37.

ference towards one's lover, prompting the birth of love in that person. The idea of the sister, Phénice, may have been borrowed, for in *Mélite* the hero, Eraste, diverts his attention (just as Damis does in Marivaux's play) to Chloris, sister of Tircis, who has fallen in love with Mélite, former mistress of Eraste. In Corneille's play, however, the feigned indifference mentioned above does not have any effect, since Mélite will marry Tircis, and Eraste will wed Chloris.

It may be said, then, that *Les Serments indiscrets* bears a direct relationship only with certain *moliéresque* sources that the dramatist had used previously. His reliance on them, when it occurs, does not improve his play because he is either unable or unwilling to employ Molière's procedure, which always so effectively marries content to style. The sense of urgency and of impending catastrophe, which emerges from the swiftness of Molière's dialogue in scenes in which spite appears to be about to conquer love, lends to these episodes a measure of suspense, and therefore of interest, which is lacking from the much longer and more involved speeches of the characters of Marivaux. In fact, long speeches usually denote calculation and the ability to deliberate, neither of which goes hand in hand with the youthful fault of spite. There is, then, a dichotomy between the essential characteristics of Marivaux's personages, characteristics in which he would have us believe, and their power to express, indeed to dissect, their most hidden feelings as full-fledged psychologists or outside, observing psychiatrists might be able to do. The close and subtle analysis of which Lucile and Damis are capable contradicts both their chronological age and the spitefulness that they would like to exhibit. Even further impoverished by the five-act length, *Les Serments indiscrets* seems, then, in its hyperdevelopment of the marivaldian frequently-stated truism that "notre coeur se moque de nos résolutions," (II, 10) monotonous and irritating. Besides, this truism is proven poorly because the heart of the characters takes too long to declare itself, and the delays are replete with hair-splitting arguments, that denote that the *résolutions* count more than they should. This is also the opinion of Marcel Arland, otherwise an admirer of Marivaux: "L'action languit, les héros nous agacent par leur bavardage et leurs petites crispations; s'ils refusent de céder à leur amour, ce n'est plus par une pudeur touchante, mais par le point d'honneur le plus vain; c'est surtout pour que la pièce existe, et prenne les dimensions d'une tragédie."[14] Had Marivaux been able to follow also the stylistic procedures of his seventeenth-century predecessor, that is, had he been able to have his characters' words betray more adequately their youth and

[14]Arland, in Marivaux's *Théâtre* (Paris: Librairie Gallimard, 1949), xlviii.

their spite, perhaps no one would have been able to liken *Les Serments indiscrets* to a tragedy.

The only modern revival of the comedy occurred in 1956. This corroborates the validity of the poor reception it had some two decades ago. Guy Dupur, for example, wrote:

> Jamais peut-être, Marivaux n'a fait preuve d'une telle imagination que dans cette oeuvre où l'imagination n'est rien. On ne sait s'il veut démontrer la vanité de l'amour ou la vanité du langage. Pris au piège des mots, ses personnages en sont à la fois les victimes, et les défenseurs. Car leur amour n'existerait pas sans les mots qu'ils utilisent et l'on nous prouve, à force de mots, que ce langage est soumis à tant de contradictions, à tant d'emplois différents qu'il ne sert a rien.[15]

Repetition and overstatement are, almost always, taboo on the stage. But if they prove lack of imagination, they do not contradict good memory. Good, but not excellent, for if Marivaux had recollected also the *moliéresque* expression of spite, his effort might have been approved.

---

[15]Quoted by Greene in *Marivaux*, 148; source not given.

L'ECOLE DES MERES

If failures, or semifailures, always greeted Marivaux at the Théâtre Français, it was, as shown above, partly because his recollections of Molière were either limited or differently treated. With *L'Ecole des mères*, however, the eighteenth-century dramatist appears to abandon the pretense of total originality, and he relies heavily, indeed, on the seventeenth-century master. The title itself brings to mind *L'Ecole des maris* and *L'Ecole des femmes*, but there are also reminiscences of *L'Avare*.

In Marivaux's comedy, Madame Argante is an austere mother who educates her daughter, Angélique, in cloistered fashion. She watches her movements, even her dress; and in practically no area does she give her daughter any freedom of choice. Among other things, she has decided to have her marry the wealthy sexagenarian Damis rather than Eraste, a young man whom she loves, such decision being taken by her, of course, with the best of intentions, for she desires to spare her daughter any possible exposure to the instability of a younger husband. Lisette and Frontin, the servants, do their best to convince Madame Argante that Angélique is unhappy about the arrangements she has made. However, she misinterprets their warnings, and each subtle accusation takes on for her the aura of a compliment addressed to the rigid upbringing to which she has submitted Angélique. Damis, on the other hand, whose real name turns out to be Orgon (he had changed his name because he wanted to keep his marriage plans hidden from his son), is soon disabused by the servants. Moreover, finding out that his rival is none other than Eraste, his son, he decides to withdraw without hard feelings; whereas Madame Argante, infuriated, has no choice but to acquiesce. Eraste will marry Angélique, and the play ends with entertainers singing and dancing in typical Théâtre Italien fashion.

Angélique's incipient revolt, from its beginning to the moment of victory, provides for scenes that attempt to *educate* the mother, just as most of the episodes in *L'Ecole des maris* helped to *educate* Sganarelle. Several critics saw the relationship between Marivaux's play and that of Molière, but to date no textual comparisons have been made. Marcel Arland, for example, devoted only one line to the topic.[1] Kenneth N. McKee elaborated only very slightly: "There are certain aspects of *L'Ecole des mères* that recall Molière — this, in spite of Marivaux's avowed dislike for the type of play Molière wrote. Even granting that Marivaux added his own inimitable touch, it seems improbable that he would have written *L'Ecole des mères* without the materials of *L'Ecole*

[1]Arland, *Marivaux*, 142.

des femmes, L'Ecole des maris and *L'Avare*."[2] E. J. H. Greene chose to discount the relationship in one brief paragraph.[3] On the contrary, close perusal of the two comedies reveals numerous situations and much vocabulary that are similar. Space limitations make it impossible to cite them all, but a few should suffice.

It will be recalled that Sganarelle, the jealous tutor and projected husband of Isabelle, prepares the latter for the marriage to which he aspires. According to him, honesty in a girl requires very modest dress: "Que d'une serge honnête elle ait son vêtement, / Et ne porte le noir qu'aux bons jours seulement" (I, 2); later he explains:

> Oh! trois et quarte fois béni soit cet édit
> Par qui des vêtements le luxe est interdit! . . .
> Oh! que je sais au roi bon gré de ces décris! (II, 9)

Likewise, in *L'Ecole des mères*, Madame Argante has her daughter dress in what she, the mother, considers proper clothing. And Angélique complains: "Voyez, je vous prie, de quel air on m'habille! suis-je vêtue comme une autre? regardez comme me voilà faite! Ma mère appelle cela un habit modeste . . . Je ne porte pas de rubans" (Scene 5).

In another situation Isabelle sends a letter to Valère in which she analyzes this daring act: "Ce n'est pas la contrainte où je me trouve qui a fait naître les sentiments que j'ai pour vous; mais c'est elle qui en précipite le témoignage, et qui me fait passer sur des formalités où la bienséance du sexe oblige" (II, 8). Similarly, Angélique explains to Eraste the cause of her inability to hide her feelings, or at least to postpone their eloquent expression.

> Si ma mère m'avait donné plus d'expérience, si j'avais été un peu dans le monde, je vous aimerais peut-être sans vous le dire; je vous ferais languir pour le savoir; je retiendrais mon coeur; cela n'irait pas si vite, et vous m'auriez déjà dit que je suis une ingrate; mais je ne saurais la contrefaire. Mettez-vous à ma place; j'ai tant souffert de contrainte, ma mère m'a rendu la vie si triste! j'ai eu si peu satisfaction, elle a tant mortifié mes sentiments! Je suis si lasse de les cacher, que, lorsque je suis contente, et que je le puis dire, je l'ai déjà dit avant que de savoir que j'ai parlé; c'est comme quelqu'un qui respire. (Scene 18)

Worthy of note is that both girls blame the *contrainte* in which they were raised for their present actions. Moreover, both Angélique and Isabelle have thought out the same explanation, and they both offer it to their lovers.

There are many other comparisons to be made between *L'Ecole des maris* and *L'Ecole des mères*. Angélique and Isabelle go through similar moments of submission and revolt. The latter submits to her tutor

---

[2]McKee, *Theater of Marivaux*, 160-161.
[3]Greene, *Marivaux*, 148-149.

before the beginning of the play, as is apparent from the exposition[4] and also throughout the unfolding of the events on stage. Likewise, Angélique submits not only before the curtain, but repeatedly during the whole play.[5] Moreover, Angélique's mutiny in parts of *L'Ecole des mères*, though expressed more mildly, may be likened to the moments of revolt in which Isabelle engages in *L'Ecole des maris*, more directly and more forcefully. Isabelle's complaint to Léonore regarding Sganarelle's behavior, "C'est un miracle encore qu'il ne m'ait aujourd'hui enfermée à la clef" (I, 2), may have been at the source of Angélique's revolt, which she words to Lisette: "N'être jamais qu'avec elle, n'entendre que des préceptes qui me lassent, ne faire que des lectures qui m'ennuient, est-ce là le moyen d'avoir de l'esprit? qu'est-ce que cela apprend? Il y a des petites filles de sept ans qui sont plus avancées que moi. Cela n'est-il pas ridicule? . . . Si je n'avais pas le coeur bon, je crois que je haïrais ma mère d'être cause que j'ai des émotions pour des choses dont je suis sûre que je ne me soucierais pas si je les avais" (Scene 6).
    Isabelle's plot to contact Valère,

Je fais, pour une fille, un projet bien hardi;
Mais l'injuste rigueur dont envers moi l'on use,
Dans tout esprit bien fait me servira d'excuse (II, 1)

is probably at the root of Scene 7 in Marivaux's play, in which Angélique sees Eraste in hiding, despite her mother's instructions. The only difference is that Isabelle uses Sganarelle as her messenger in contacting Valère, "J'en veux, dans les fers où je suis prisonnière, / Hasarder un qui parle avec plus de lumière" (II, 5), and in fact does so with extreme audacity: "*Elle fait semblant d'embrasser Sganarelle, et donne sa main à baiser à Valère*" (II, 14), whereas it would never even occur to Angélique to go so far. Actually, Isabelle, like Agnès,[6] is consistently more brazen than her eighteenth-century counterpart. A speech such as the following, in which her plotting goes so far as engendering an elopement,

Oui, le trépas cent fois me semble à craindre
Que cet hymen fatal où l'on veut me contraindre;
Et tout ce que je fais pour en fuir ses rigueurs
Doit trouver quelques grâces auprès de mes censeurs.

----

[4]See Act I, Scenes 1 and 2.
    [5]Lisette, describing Angélique to her mother: "Vous savez qu'à peine ose-t-elle lever les yeux, tant elle a peur de sortir de cette modestie sévère que vous voulez qu'elle ait" (Scene 4); Angélique to her mother: "Je ferai tout ce qu'il vous plaira, ma mère" (Scene 5); Angélique to Lisette: "Quand ma mère me parle, je n'ai plus d'esprit" (Scene 6); Angélique to Eraste: "On m'a dit qu'il fallait être plus retenue dans les discours qu'on tient à son amant" (Scene 18).
    [6]See following discussion.

> Le temps presse, il fait nuit; allons, sans crainte aucune,
> A la foi d'un amant commettre ma fortune. (III, 1)

would have been beyond Angélique's capacity for mutiny. On the contrary, when revolt is to be expressed more freely in Marivaux's play, it is the servant, Lisette, who says the words her mistress perhaps thinks of but certainly does not have the audacity to express. Thus, as will be shown in the comparison with *L'Ecole des femmes*, Marivaux's heroine suggests a retrogression: more cautious, more sedate, more timid and ever conscious of her duty to proper social decorum, Angélique lacks the engaging color and brisk sprightliness of Isabelle.

A further rapport exists between Molière's Ariste and Marivaux's Damis. Ariste is an elderly suitor, but he understands the aspirations of youth, and he does not force the girl he loves into any step she might dislike; likewise, as mentioned, Damis, the elderly suitor of Angélique, complies with the wishes of the young girl.

Sganarelle's counterpart is, of course, Madame Argante. The limitations to which Molière's hero submits Isabelle in Act I, Scene 2, in Act II, Scene 9, and in other instances too numerous to mention here, are synthesized by Madame Argante's instructions to her daughter. These, although almost as numerous, are packed by her into the following significant speech: "Gardez ce goût de retraite, de solitude, de modestie, de pudeur qui me charme en vous; ne plaisez qu'à votre mari" (Scene 5).

Of course, some of the materials of *L'Ecole des maris* are not original with Molière: the latter may have used Terence's *Adelphoe*, the *Décameron* of Boccaccio, *La Folle gageure* of Boisrobert, and Dorimond's *La Femme industrieuse*.[7] Yet none of the passages that influenced Marivaux has been borrowed by Molière from his predecessors. These seem to be original and of Molière's invention.[8] It is therefore safe to assume that Marivaux's direct source was *L'Ecole des maris*.

Turning to *L'Ecole des femmes*, the role of Agnès leads to the exploration of another area of the Marivaux-Molière relationship. Of course, many of the characters of the seventeeth-century dramatist had become standard types for a number of eighteenth-century playwrights, and some were referred to time and again in novels as well. Marivaux himself invites a comparison when he has Frontin assert, "Angélique est une Agnès élevée dans la plus sévère contrainte" (Scene 2). The author appears to have been thinking often of Molière's comedy as he

---

[7]See Lancaster, *French Dramatic Literature*, 234-235.
[8]*Ibid.*, 234.

was writing *L'Ecole des mères*, for the plays are similar in many respects.

From a general viewpoint, both comedies use the universal theme of the education of a young girl for marriage. Angélique and Agnès are brought up with severity and are taught virtues and the utility of innocence. The educators have definite aims in mind, a precise type of womanhood to which their respective pupil is expected to conform. And both educators are fooled in their expectations, in their hopes, as youth wins over tyrannic teachings.

From a specific standpoint, the similarities are so numerous that only a few need to be pointed out. For example, consider Arnolphe's description of the type of girl he wishes to marry,

> En un mot, qu'elle soit d'une ignorance extrême:
> Et c'est assez pour elle, à vous en bien parler,
> De savoir prier Dieu, m'aimer, coudre, et filer. (I, 1)

and Chrysalde's reply,

> Une femme stupide est donc votre marotte? . . .
> Mais comment voulez-vous, après tout, qu'une bête
> Puisse jamais savoir ce que c'est qu'être honnête? . . .
> Une femme d'esprit peut trahir son devoir;
> Mais il faut, pour le moins, qu'elle ose le vouloir:
> Et la stupide au sien peut manquer d'ordinaire,
> Sans en avoir l'envie et sans penser le faire. (I, 1)

that recall the upbringing of Angélique, who had to bear the severity prescribed by Madame Argante, the same upbringing causing Lisette to remark to her mistress: "Votre naïveté me fait rire," (Scene 6), and eliciting the following answer from Angélique: "Serait-ce de même si j'avais joui d'une liberté honnête? . . . J'ai des émotions pour des choses dont je suis sûre que je ne me soucierais pas si je les avais" (Scene 6). Thus Angélique feels certain bad emotions that she would not feel had she been brought up differently. What Chrysalde foresaw in the case of Agnès (that a naïve woman may be more prone to do evil than a clever one) has been crystallized in the case of Angélique.

In another scene, Arnolphe has Agnès read several *maximes de mariage:*

> Celle qu'un lien honnête
> Fait entrer au lit d'autrui,
> Doit se mettre dans la tête . . .
> Que l'homme qui la prend,
> Ne la prend que pour lui . . .
> Elle ne se doit parer . . .
> Qu'autant que peut désirer le mari . . .
> Hors ceux dont au mari la visite se rend,
> La bonne règle défend de recevoir aucune âme . . .

Ces sociétés déréglées,
Qu'on nomme belles assemblées . . .
En bonne politique
On les doit interdire . . .
Des promenades du temps,
Ou repas qu'on donne aux champs,
Il ne faut point qu'elle essaie. (III, 2)

Likewise, Madame Argante instructs her daughter in the duties of a wife: "Les vertus dont vous allez avoir besoin ne vous coûteront rien; et voici les plus essentielles: c'est, d'abord, de n'aimer que votre mari. . . . Vous n'en [en referring to friends] devez point avoir d'autres que ceux de Monsieur Damis . . . et surtout gardez ce goût de retraite, de solitude, de pudeur qui me charme en vous; ne plaisez qu'à votre mari" (Scene 5). And although it is true that Molière's *maximes de mariage* was inspired by Desmaretz's adaptation of *Saint Gregory of Nazianzen,* Marivaux did not have to go any further than to Molière, especially in view of the many other resemblances that exist between the two plays.

In addition, Agnès' letter seems to have furnished the material for many of Angélique's comments. Agnès writes: "Je ne sais comment faire . . . et je me défie de mes paroles. Comme je commence à connaître qu'on m'a toujours tenue dans l'ignorance . . . j'aurai toutes les peines du monde à me passer de vous . . . je serai bien aise d'être à vous. Peut-être qu'il y a du mal à dire cela" (III, 4). On her part, Angélique echoes: "Quand ma mère me parle, je n'ai plus d'esprit. . . . Il y a des petites filles de sept ans qui sont plus avancées que moi. . . . Vraiment oui, je l'aime, pourvu qu'il n'y ait point de mal à avouer cela; car je suis si ignorante!" (Scene 6). And later she repeats: "Je vais comme le coeur me mène . . . et s'il y a de ma faute à vous avouer si souvent que je vous aime . . ." (Scene 18). Like Agnès, then, Angélique knows that she is *ignorante;* and, like Agnès again, she does not know if it is proper to confess her love to the man of her choice.

A further similarity emerges from a comparison between Arnolphe's complaint:

Quoi! j'aurai dirigé son éducation
Avec tant de tendresse et de précaution;
Je l'aurai fait passer chez moi dès son enfance,
Et j'en aurai chéri la plus tendre espérance (IV, 1)

and Madame Argante's lament: "Ingrate! est-ce là le fruit des soins que je me suis donnés pour vous donner de la vertu? . . . Vous plaindre d'une éducation qui m'occupait toute entière" (Scene 18). Especially notable is Arnolphe's and Madame Argante's equal preoccupation with the education given, and their disappointment in seeing it fail.

The episode in which Arnolphe apostrophizes Agnès after finding
her in the company of Horace is probably at the root of a similar
admonition Madame Argante addresses to Angélique. Arnolphe says:

Ah! Ah! si jeune encore, vous jouez de ces tours! . . .
Et vous savez donner des rendez-vous la nuit,
Ah! coquine, en venir à cette perfidie!
Malgré tous mes bienfaits former un tel dessein!
Petit serpent que j'ai réchauffé dans mon sein. (V, 4)

Likewise, after finding her daughter in the company of Eraste, Madame
Argante accuses, "Ménager des intrigues à mon insu," which corresponds to Arnolphe's *vous jouez de ces tours* and which expresses with
similar eloquence the disbelief and grief of Agnès' tutor.

Of course, the education of children by parents and tutors had
supplied playwrights with suitable comic material even before Molière
and certainly during the time between Molière's death and the beginning of Marivaux's theatrical career. Yet, there is little question here of
mere coincidences. The critics are unanimous concerning the validity
of the *rapprochement* between *L'Ecole des mères* and *L'Ecole des
femmes:* Ferdinand Brunetière, for example, whose comments on the
subject have been quoted in the Introduction; Gustave Larroumet, who
wrote, "*L'Ecole des mères* s'inspire évidemment de *L'Ecole des
femmes,*"[9] and who later called Marivaux's heroine "Une soeur de
l'Agnès de Molière";[10] Marcel Arland, who commented, "Il va de soi
que, dans cette pièce, Marivaux s'inspire de *l'Ecole des Femmes*";[11]
Jean Fleury, who went even further when he declared, "*L'Ecole des
mères* est une sorte de réduction de *l'Ecole des Femmes,* dans laquelle
Arnolphe a changé de sexe, et où la mère a remplacé le tuteur
amoureux";[12] Arthur Tilley, who confirmed also, "Its title, *L'Ecole des
mères,* is reminiscent of Molière";[13] and even Kenneth N. McKee, who
admitted the *moliéresque* influence,[14] as did E. J. H. Greene, "The
title, the problem, Frontin's remark . . . everything suggested that here
was a Molière theme brought up to date."[15]

Granted the unanimity of critics in so far as the identification of the
source, there is, nevertheless, much lack of agreement both with
respect to plagiarism versus an acceptable degree of imitation, and with
respect to the degree to which Agnès was refashioned into the character

[9]Larroumet, *Marivaux, sa vie et ses oeuvres,* 156.
[10]*Ibid.,* 207.
[11]Arland, in Marivaux's *Théâtre,* 1551.
[12]Fleury, *Marivaux et le marivaudage,* 110.
[13]Tilley, *Three French Dramatists,* 103.
[14]See earlier discussion.
[15]Greene, *Marivaux,* 148.

of Angélique. For example, Brunetière's words, "a voulu refaire," are taken to task by Kenneth N. McKee, who objected:

> The verb "a voulu" seems inappropriate, for it implies that Marivaux set out deliberately to rewrite Molière's comedies in much the same manner as Voltaire tried to rewrite Crébillon's tragedies. Nothing could have been farther from Marivaux's mind. Our knowledge of his dislike for Molière's plays and his peaceful disposition forbids our attributing to him a churlish jealousy of Molière. Both plays deal with the recurrent theme of a young girl enlightened by love, rebelling against parental or tutorial severity. If occasional facets of *L'Ecole des femmes* reappear in *L'Ecole des mères*, it is not necessarily by deliberate plagiarism, but rather because the two plays naturally revolve about certain common human verities. Furthermore, if Brunetière had wanted to prove Marivaux dependent on Molière, he should have cited *L'Ecole des maris* and *L'Avare* along with *L'Ecole des femmes*.[16]

Although Brunetière's choice of words does indeed suggest deliberate imitation on the part of Marivaux, knowledge of the playwright's dislike for Molière is only an indirect one, and dislike *per se* does not prohibit, necessarily, using stock episodes of a predecessor's invention in order to improve one's own chances for success. Moreover, there is no rapport between one's *peaceful disposition* and one's ability to steer clear of celebrated *moliéresque* details that audiences simply gobbled up. Likewise, McKee's assertion that Brunetière should have pointed also to Marivaux's dependence on *L'Ecole des maris* and *L'Avare*, true so far as it goes, proves only that the nineteenth-century critic chose, for reasons unknown, to mention only the more salient source, *L'Ecole des femmes*, and does not detract at all from Brunetière's perspicacity.

In his attempt to play down the influence of Molière, McKee repeated the questionable comments of a number of previous reviewers who saw in Angélique a modernized and different Agnès. He wrote: "It must be stated, however, that Marivaux has brought Angélique up to date; Agnès is the innocent sheltered *jeune fille* of the seventeenth century, emboldened by love, whereas Angélique, though innocent and sheltered, reveals a keen intelligence and an analytical mind, not discernible in Agnès; to this she adds a flair for ruses."[17] The above represents a synthesis of other like comparisons little supported by the texts in question. Clément Caraguel, for example, an almost forgotten critic and admirer of Marivaux, declared: "Ce sont bien deux ingénues: mais Agnès est une fille du dix-septième siècle, au lieu qu'Angélique est clairement du dix-huitième . . . , et c'est en cela que consiste l'originalité de Marivaux."[18] Francisque Sarcey commented in similar

[16]McKee, *Theater of Marivaux*, 162-163.
[17]*Ibid.*, 161.
[18]Clément Caraguel, "Marivaux," *Journal des Débats* (Paris), 14 January 1860, p. 4.

fashion: "Elle [Angélique] raisonne, analyse, discute, juge. Agnès se contente d'exhaler sa plainte."[19] And Jean Fleury agreed: "Agnès est naïve parce qu'elle ne se doute pas qu'elle l'est. Angélique sait qu'elle est naïve; elle le dit, elle analyse sa naïveté, elle explique à Lisette ce que sa mère aurait dû faire, quelles seront plus tard les conséquences de ce qu'elle a fait."[20] Marcel Arland went a step further in attempting to explain: "Agnès est l'éclatant chef-d'oeuvre d'une innocence qui confine à la sottise; infiniment plus nuancée et vraisemblable, Angélique, toute innocente, connaît son innocence; le mal, elle en ignore les formes et les approches; mais qu'il existe, tout le lui montre . . . Elle se débat dans sa prison."[21] And E. J. H. Greene, suspicious though he might have been in the case of L'Ecole des mères, nevertheless could not bring himself to the point of contradicting previous critical opinion; but his doubts concerning the alleged modernity of Angélique are apparent: "If Angélique is much more discerning, much more aware of the complexities of human behaviour than Agnès, if she seems more 'modern,' it is because Marivaux was writing in a different social context. Angélique, despite the constraints she suffers, knows that other people enjoy a larger, freer life, and although her mother's presence paralyzes her, at other times she expresses her eagerness to take the risks of freedom and assume the responsibility for her own decisions."[22] On the contrary, Arthur Tilley hinted at his disagreement, "But if Angélique is less naïve than her predecessor, she is just as innocent."[23]

However, most of the above statements concerning the relationship between Agnès and Angélique are almost identical: they all consider Angélique to be the eighteenth-century counterpart of Agnès. Marcel Arland and Kenneth N. McKee bestow on Marivaux's heroine the added qualities of intelligence and analytical abilities, as well as the debatable distinction of possessing a *flair for ruses*. They also imply that Agnès was not intelligent, that she could not analyze the situation she was in and, moreover, that she was not shrewd. As a matter of fact, Marcel Arland's statement makes the point that Agnès' innocence *confine à la sottise* — which is a valid assertion if one recalls that Agnès "demande si l'on fait les enfants par l'oreille" (V, 4), but which could also be applied to Angélique who admits that "Il y a des petites filles de sept ans qui sont plus avancées que moi" (Scene 6), because a seven-year-old might share Agnès' view regarding the origin of babies.

[19]Francisque Sarcey, *Le Temps* (Paris), December 1878, p. 1.
[20]Fleury, *Marivaux et le marivaudage*, 111.
[21]Arland, *Marivaux*, 142.
[22]Greene, *Marivaux*, 149.
[23]Tilley, *Three French Dramatists*, 104.

However, with regard to Agnès' alleged lack of intelligence, of analytical ability, and of shrewdness, Molière's text gives ample proof to the contrary. Agnès' letter to Horace, in which she declares, "Comme je commence à connaître qu'on m'a toujours tenue dans l'ignorance" (III, 4) is sufficient to establish the girl's inner intelligence and ability to analyze the situation she was in — else she would not make the statement, indeed she would not write the letter and plot a remedy together with Horace. But there is additional proof:

ARNOLPHE: N'est-ce rien que les soins d'élever votre enfance?

AGNES: Vous avez là-dedans bien opéré vraiment,
        Et m'avez fait en tout instruire joliment!
        Croit-on que je me flatte, et qu'enfin, dans ma tête,
        Je ne juge pas bien que je suis une bête?
        Moi-même j'en ai honte; et dans l'âge où je suis
        Je ne veux plus passer pour sotte, si je puis. (V, 4)

Nowhere in Marivaux's play is Angélique's revolt against ignorance stronger than that of Agnès; nor is Angélique any more conscious of the exact state of her mind than Agnès is.

As to the *flair for ruses*, Agnès possessed it to a greater degree than Angélique, else she would not have managed to escape Arnolphe's vigilance and attempted to elope with Horace (V, 2). As a matter of fact, Agnès' shrewdness and *esprit* are the subject of several lines spoken by Horace to Arnolphe:

Mais ce qui m'a surpris, et qui va vous surprendre,
C'est un autre incident que vous allez entendre;
Un trait hardi qu'a fait cette jeune beauté,
Et qu'on n'attendrait point de sa simplicité. (III, 4)

The *trait hardi* refers to the letter Agnès managed to remit to Horace. This letter is the source of such astonishment,

D'une telle action n'êtes-vous pas surpris?
. . . .
Que dites-vous du tour et de ce mot d'écrit?
Euh! n'admirez-vous point cette adresse d'esprit?
(III, 4)

that the only possible conclusion is that Agnès possessed an *adresse d'esprit* uncommon in innocent, sheltered young girls of the seventeenth century.

Contrasting then, the results of Agnès' *flair for ruses* with Angélique's plotting merely to see Eraste without her mother's consent, the latter's action appears mild, almost insignificant. Despite the fact that both girls have their moments of quiet submission and of active rebellion, Agnès and not Angélique is the one who is less submissive and more mutinous. Indeed some of her acts of disobedience (sending the letter to Horace, attempting to elope) are not only uncommon with innocent, sheltered young girls of Molière's time but are rather indicative of a type of behavior more frequent in the society of the twentieth century. How far from such behavior are the actions of Angélique! It thus seems confining to label Agnès an "innocent sheltered *jeune fille* of the seventeenth century, emboldened by love." Chances are that if she were simply that, she and the play would not have survived. Agnès' extreme disobedience, ability to plot and to *get* her way constitute not only the possible result of a severe education but represent, on a larger scale, the eternal struggle between youth and old age, between *les anciens et les modernes* on the domestic level.

The details of this struggle, the boldness with which Agnès fights, and the tongue-lashing she administers to Arnolphe offset the sporadic, infantile, submissive behavior of this character without, nevertheless, diminishing the ambiguity that provides for the undying interest one has in her. Agnès of the *scène du ruban* and the later Agnès, that of Act III, Scene 4 and Act V, Scene 4 for example, denote a disquieting dualism one does not find in Marivaux's heroine; Agnès supplies the disturbing realization that extremes (obedience, utmost docility, naïve innocence) go sometimes hand in hand with opposing extremes (disobedience, clearcut impudence, sin). On the contrary, Angélique lacks this dualism. She is a more logical character: never too disobedient nor too obedient, but certainly never impudent or totally rebellious. Angélique, more consistent in her behavior than Agnès, is less human than her predecessor and consequently less believable because she fails to make the spectator uneasy. Marivaux placed his heroine on the path of the *juste milieu* Molière apparently preached but never quite practiced in the depiction of his best characters.[24] And the *juste milieu* is not, generally, the path walked by the average teenager.

On the other hand, the ambiguity of Agnès, her innocence and her teen-age female shrewdness and independence belong not only to the seventeenth century but also to the eighteenth and indeed to the twentieth. Compared to her, Angélique is not merely a pale copy of Agnès but also a character lacking the scope of her predecessor and thus representing not an "Agnès brought up to date" but rather a regressive type of docile and sporadically rebellious youth that Agnès seemed to have irremediably interred.

Marivaux's reliance on Molière extends also to *L'Avare*. Kenneth N. McKee saw the relationship when he wrote, "The father-son rivalry in *L'Ecole des mères* savors of the Harpagon-Cléante situation in *L'Avare*, except that Eraste is not disrespectful toward his father, as Cléante had

---

[24]He did, of course, depict dull personages following the *juste milieu:* Chrysalde, for example.

been toward Harpagon."[25] Textual comparisons reveal the fact that the rivalry between Monsieur Damis and Eraste never is exaggerated by Marivaux, and that the essential goodness of all Marivaux's fathers is seen in Monsieur Damis, who cedes his place graciously to Eraste. This type of father-son rivalry savors also of the rivalry between Monsieur Grifon and Valère in Regnard's *La Sérénade;* in the latter play, however, as in *L'Avare,* the father cedes his place to the son only after much ado and when he has no other choice left; in both plays, the mother is portrayed by a Madame Argante, and the character of Champagne also is found in the two comedies.

Because the *moliéresque* influence prevailed, practically no one bothered to point to other possible sources. Pierre Duviquet opined that Angélique's words, "J'aimerais mieux être sa femme seulement huit jours, que de l'être toute ma vie de l'autre,"[26] are an imitation, as far as form is concerned, of the following verses of an epigram by Jean-Baptiste Rousseau.

> J'aimerais mieux, pour le bien de mon âme,
> Avoir affaire à dix filles par mois
> Que de toucher en dix ans une femme.

It is highly improbable and certainly impossible to prove that Marivaux had reference to Jean-Baptiste Rousseau, for the expression of the thought in question, in similar form, is not unusual in either prose or verse (since antitheses are often the "pets" of writers). In addition, E. J. H. Greene pointed to Number 12 of *Le Spectateur français* in which Marivaux also is concerned with a girl's education at the hands of a bigoted mother. The critic maintained that *L'Ecole des mères* is, in part, based on the moralist's concern for the nefarious influence of a mother's piety on the upbringing of her daughter.[27] It will be recalled that Marivaux's own daughter became a nun, but the dramatist could not bring to the stage religious considerations that were entirely taboo, and thus he was constrained to place himself, more or less, in the footsteps of Molière. A close reading of Number 12 of *Le Spectateur français,* however, does not reveal any specific similarities, and it must be concluded, therefore, that Marivaux's previous contribution on the subject is only remotely connected, if at all, with *L'Ecole des mères.*

Marivaux's twentieth play, then, although written against the background of considerable experience both at the Théâtre Français and the Théâtre Italien, not only is not devoid of *moliéresque* detail, but is replete with situations and vocabulary attributable beyond question to

---

[25]McKee, *Theater of Marivaux,* 162.
[26]Duviquet, ed., *Oeuvres complètes,* 4, 443.
[27]Greene, *Marivaux,* 149.

Molière. The powers of inventiveness of the eighteenth-century play-wright, who was then at the height of his career, while adequate, continue to show the need of supportive *moliéresque* scenes. If one keeps in mind the fact that, in other instances in which the recollections were more limited or differently treated, the results often bordered on failure, there is no surprise that *L'Ecole des mères* had a very good critical reception in the eighteenth century and enjoyed a most respectable fourteen-day consecutive run. Although today, superficially, one might conclude that the matter of the education of a young girl in general, and of her preparation for marriage in particular, has lost much of the urgency that it commanded in Marivaux's time (which would make of *L'Ecole des mères* a museum piece rather than a play worthy of contemporary stage production), it is relevant to recall that *L'Ecole des mères*, in its twentieth-century Odéon revival, received considerable acclaim. Marivaux's treatment of ingenuity in a young girl, *moliéresque* as it is, cannot help but bestow on the play a sempiternal timeliness.

L'HEUREUX STRATAGÈME

In spite of the fact that *L'Heureux stratagème* is another of Marivaux's *surprise* plays, few commentators have suggested a comparison between it and a Molière comedy. As it happened in the case of other plays by Marivaux, it was a Molière specialist, Georges Lafenestre, who detected the influence of *La Princesse d'Elide* on the eighteenth-century playwright's reworking of the theme of disdained love. But he wrote merely: "*La Princesse d'Elide* lui fournit des scènes assez nombreuses dans . . . *L'Heureux stratagème,*"[1] and he suggested no corroborative textual examples. The same lack of elaboration is found in Xavier de Courville's staccato remark, "Marivaux, dans *L'Heureux stratagème,* suivra plus près encore que dans *La Surprise* le sujet de Molière et de Moreto."[2] The already considered *El Desdén con el desdén* of Moreto, which did not influence Marivaux's other surprise plays, has no direct relationship with *L'Heureux stratagème* either. As pointed out before, the subject of feigned indifference of lovers towards one another, which one finds in the Spanish work, might indeed be at the source of *La Princesse d'Elide;* whereas Marivaux could not have had any reason to go so far back as Moreto's effort especially since Molière's comedy, to a greater or lesser degree, is present in so many of his dramatic compositions.

Nevertheless, constant in his belief in D'Alembert's reports concerning Marivaux's alleged dislike for Molière and alleged unwillingness to imitate the seventeenth-century playwright, Kenneth N. McKee did not even mention *La Princesse d'Elide.* While praising the originality of *L'Heureux stratagème* (more about which later), he noted simply that, "Perhaps the characters and plot of *L'Heureux stratagème* are not too far removed from other comedies of the day."[3] Of course, the comedies of the day, including some of those of Marivaux, were replete with *moliéresque* themes, not the least reworked of which was in fact that of spite, of withheld, misdirected, and finally redirected and declared love. E. J. H. Greene mentioned specifically *La Princesse d'Elide*, but only in passing and in order to discard it as a possible source. He commented, "The most frequent critical reaction has been to dismiss the play as an imitation of Molière's *La Princesse d'Elide*, or of Riccoboni's 1717 version of Moreto's *Dédain contre Dédain*. The element of amorous spite is present in all three, therefore etc. But this is merely to 'deal with' a work by attaching it to another and thus

[1]Lafenestre, *Molière*, 192-193.
[2]Xavier de Courville, *Le Théâtre de Marivaux* (Paris: Droz, 1943), 1, 66.
[3]McKee, *Theater of Marivaux*, 171.

classifying it. It is much simpler, and no doubt nearer the truth, to presume no other sources than Marivaux's mastery of his craft."[4] In point of fact, it appears incorrect to refer to a possible cabalistic vogue of relating *L'Heureux stratagème* to *La Princesse d'Elide* or to *Dédain contre Dédain*, for few indeed have been those reviewers who have been *guilty*, to date, of such a *rapprochement*. In addition to which, classification of a work is a time-honored critical procedure the validity of which resides in the possibility it affords for better comprehension and appreciation. On the other hand, the presumption that Marivaux's mastery of his craft is at the sole source of *L'Heureux stratagème* seems simplistic, because a close reading of it and *La Princesse d'Elide* reveals similarities worth noting, and corroborates once more Marivaux's on-again, off-again, reliance upon Molière's farce.

The plot of the comedy is built around a *chassé-croisé*: the Countess and Dorante are in love and have been for a while. When boredom sets in, the attention of the Countess is diverted to the Chevalier. The latter had been the friend of the Marquise, but he is now being lured away. The Marquise, more mature, if cold-blooded, views the situation stoically and calculates that a stratagem of pretending to be in love with Dorante will reawaken the Countess' love for him. As soon as spite runs its course, the plot succeeds. In fact it succeeds so well that a notary soon arrives with marriage contracts for Dorante and the Marquise, and the Countess and the Chevalier, respectively. However, in the final moments just preceding the signing ceremony, the parties retract; Dorante will marry the Countess, and the Marquise will put the Chevalier on a six-month probationary period, at the end of which she will decide if he is worthy of her hand.

Act III, Scene 2 of Molière's comedy contains an episode that is probably the source of Act II, Scene 2 and Act III, Scene 4 of Marivaux's play. It will be recalled that Euryale finds it extremely difficult to continue to feign indifference vis-à-vis the Princess. At times his love is stronger than the strategy he promised to undertake, "J'ai pensé plus de vingt fois oublier ma résolution, pour me jeter à ses pieds, et lui faire un aveu sincère de l'ardeur que je sens pour elle" (III, 2). At this point Moron intervenes and encourages Euryale: "Donnez-vous-en bien de garde, seigneur, si vous m'en voulez croire. Vous avez trouvé la meilleure invention du monde, et je me trompe fort si elle ne vous réussit. . . . Demeureuz ferme, au moins, dans le chemin que vous avez pris" (III, 2). Likewise, Marivaux's Dorante is so much in love that he is unable to carry out his plan of pretending to ignore the Countess. He hesitates, vacillates, and is often at a loss as to what to

[4]Greene, *Marivaux*, 158-159.

say or what gestures to make. And, like Moron, the Marquise has to persuade Dorante of the necessity of pursuing the plan until the Countess' attention is returned entirely to him, "Je vous dis que si vous tenez bon, vous la verrez pleurer de douleur. . . . Je ne réponds de rien, si vous n'allez jusque là" (II, 2). Nevertheless, later Dorante wavers again, and then the following dialogue takes place between himself and the Marquise.

DORANTE: Vous voyez combien elle [the Countess] est agitée.

LA MARQUISE: Et vous brûlez d'envie de vous rendre!

DORANTE: Me siérait-il de faire le cruel?

LA MARQUISE: Nous touchons au terme, et nous manquons notre coup si vous allez si vite . . . allons jusqu'au contrat, comme nous l'avons résolu; ce moment seul décidera si on vous aime. Tenez bon jusqu'à cette épreuve, pour l'intérêt de votre amour même. (III, 4)

Thus Dorante's hesitation reflects that of Euryale, whereas the Marquise's advice, *tenez bon,* echoes Moron's *demeurez ferme.* Such similarities hardly could be said to be coincidental.

There are additional resemblances that can be pointed out between the two comedies under discussion. Euryale administers the *coup de grâce* to the Princess in the following manner:

Car enfin . . . madame . . . je ne feindrai point de vous dire que l'amour aujourd'hui s'est rendu maître de mon coeur, et qu'une des princesses vos cousines, l'aimable et belle Aglante, a renversé d'un coup d'oeil tous les projets de ma fierté. . . . Il faut que ce miracle éclate aux yeux de tout le monde, et nous ne devons point différer à nous rendre tous deux contents. Pour moi, madame, je vous sollicite de vos suffrages, pour obtenir celle que je souhaite. (IV, 1)

Likewise, in Marivaux's play, Dorante announces his marriage to the Marquise and, like Euryale, he also begs the approval of the woman he really loves, "Oui, Comtesse, Madame [the Marquise] me fait l'honneur de me donner sa main; et comme nous sommes chez vous, nous venons vous prier de permettre qu'on nous y unisse" (III, 10).

Later in Molière's play, Euryale confesses the *feinte* he had displayed so far and excuses it: "Je n'ai jamais aimé que vous . . . et tout ce que j'ai pu vous dire n'a été qu'une feinte . . . que je n'ai suivie qu'avec toutes les violences imaginables" (V, 2). In Marivaux's comedy, the dialogue that closes the play reproduces faithfully the movement of Euryale's speech:

LA COMTESSE: Quoi! Dorante à mes genoux?

DORANTE: Et plus pénétré d'amour qu'il ne le fut jamais.

LA COMTESSE: . . . Dorante m'aime donc encore?

DORANTE: Et n'a jamais cessé d'aimer que vous.

LA COMTESSE: Comment avez-vous pu feindre si longtemps?

DORANTE: Je ne l'ai pu qu'à force d'amour. (III, 10)

Dorante's *Et n'a jamais cessé de vous aimer* corresponds to Euryale's *Je n'ai jamais aimé que vous,* whereas *Je ne l'ai pu qu'à force d'amour* repeats the idea expressed by Euryale's *une feinte . . . que je n'ai suivie qu'avec toutes les violences imaginables*.

Critics have pointed to only two other possible sources of influence for *L'Heureux stratagème*. Pierre Duviquet noted simply that the Countess' line "Je défiais son coeur de me manquer jamais" (III, 4) is an imitation of Oreste's line in Racine's *Andromaque,* "Je défiais ses yeux de me tromper jamais" (I, 1), but this is probably an involuntary recollection.[5] At any rate, *Andromaque* provided no other source for *L'Heureux stratagème*. Jean Fleury stated that some influence must have been exercised by Lope de Vega's *Le Chien du jardinier,* which deals with approximately the same topic as *El Désden con el désden* and *La Princesse d'Elide*.[6] However, there are no specific similarities between Lope's play and that of Marivaux, and the influence, if any, was surely an indirect one, Molière probably acting as the transmitter.

The instances of similarity notwithstanding, Marivaux departs somewhat from the theme furnished by Molière: he deals with adult love, whereas Molière dealt with young love; in Marivaux's play the Countess is mature enough to be sorry for and confess her mistakes at the end of the play, whereas in *La Princesse d'Elide* the heroine demands time in order to decide if she will marry Euryale; in *L'Heureux stratagème,* at the final curtain, the Marquise and the Chevalier have not found happiness yet, whereas in Molière's comedy Aglante is promised the hand of one of the two other princes and, although the play ends before Aglante actually marries, she is such a pale figure in the plot that the question of her happiness is not nearly so important as that of the Marquise. In addition, there are some typically marivaldian lines that denote the maturity or at least the aging process undergone by some of the characters. For example, the Countess' regretful cry: "Misérable amour-propre de femme! Misérable vanité d'être aimée!" (III, 6). Such an expression of remorse is particularly noteworthy since it constitutes a total reversal from the more youthful and flirtatious pose that she had displayed in the beginning of the play. Although in the first act she had made an apology of infidelity: "Eh bien! infidèle soit puisque tu veux que je le sois; crois-tu me faire peur avec ce grand mot-là . . . bien loin que l'infidélité soit un crime, c'est que je soutiens qu'il ne faut pas

[5]Duviquet, ed., *Oeuvres complètes,* 4, 583.

[6]Fleury, *Marivaux et le marivaudage,* 135.

hésiter un moment d'en faire une, quand on en est tentée, à moins que de vouloir tromper les gens, ce qu'il faut éviter, à quelque prix que ce soit" (I, 4), at the end of the comedy she laments her initial behavior and proves that she has grown into a more reasonable person, "Eh bien, mon enfant, je me trompais; je parlais d'infidélité sans la connaître" (III, 6). Moreover, other lines indicate the strong understanding Marivaux had of the feminine penchant for innovation and variety in a lover. When Dorante says, "souffrez que je vous parle de mon amour," the Countess' reply is charmingly valid, if slightly cruel, "N'est-ce que cela? Je sais votre amour par coeur" (I, 5).

Marivaux's inventiveness also may be seen in the ways in which *L'Heureux stratagème* differs from the two *Surprises*, for in the latest play both the Countess and the Marquise are independent women (unlike the heroines in the *Surprises*, who were widows whose present was conditioned by their past), free to determine their premarital behavior and to make their own conjugal arrangements unencumbered by family considerations. This slight reworking of the old theme, coupled with their unwillingness to acquiesce in the *moliéresque* influence, caused some admirers of Marivaux to compliment highly *L'Heureux stratagème*. Kenneth N. McKee, for example, wrote: "The action moves forward briskly, the dialogue is smart, the climax is well handled; on the whole, *L'Heureux stratagème* remains a splendid example of eighteenth-century light comedy."[7] E. J. H. Greene went even further, "It [*L'Heureux stratagème*] was written by a Marivaux at the height of his powers," and then he goes on to call the play a classic.[8] Such laudatory comments are indeed, and in part, corroborated by the initial review of the *Mercure de France*,[9] but it is probable that the eighteenth-century favorable reception was caused by the fact that the audiences could themselves note the celebrated *moliéresque* theme, rather than by the fact that they were pleasingly startled by the marivaldian innovations. This assumption might explain the absence of *L'Heureux stratagème* from the French theatrical repertory until its post-World War II revival by the Théâtre National Populaire. In fact, the value of the comedy has been questioned somewhat by other critics. Jean Fleury did not like the valet-soubrette intrigue,[10] and Arthur Tilley criticized the play both in general and in specific terms:

> [It] is neither so well constructed nor so entertaining. . . . This 'Happy Stratagem,' it need not be said, has the desired effect, but the manoeuvring of the four lovers which it occasions is too complicated and lasts too long. Moreover,

[7]McKee, *Theater of Marivaux*, 171.
[8]Greene, *Marivaux*, 158.
[9]*Le Mercure de France* (Paris), June 1733, pp. 1428-1441.
[10]Fleury, *Marivaux et le marivaudage*, 136.

though the Countess is a good study of the coquette who is not without heart, and the Marquise of a kind-hearted woman of society with a sense of humour, none of the characters has much individuality. The result is an ingenious game which shews off the skill of the players rather than a true representation of nature.[11]

The broad range of views concerning *L'Heureux stratagème* (a *classic* according to E. J. H. Greene, a *game* only for Arthur Tilley) is hardly conclusive, but it would seem that both labels could apply more aptly to *La Princesse d'Elide:* a classic because it was imitated so often (even by a playwright who professed to dislike Molière); a game because the chronological age of the Princess is such that *playing* is both within her character and what she does, in fact, from beginning to end, better than any of Marivaux's females whom she inspired to greater or lesser degrees.

[11]Tilley, *Three French Dramatists,* 104.

LA MÈRE CONFIDENTE

Although Marivaux was now reaching the end of his playwriting career, *La Mère confidente* still shows some *moliéresque* influence. The dramatist does not treat the conflict between mother and daughter in the same way that Molière usually dealt with the struggle between father and daughter: "As a rule, in Molière's comedies and those of his successors, the conflict is of a secondary importance and is treated as comedy. However, Marivaux not only makes this conflict the focal point of the play, but he treats the subject with a sympathetic tenderness that was startingly new on the French stage in 1735."[1] The newness referred to is that this play could be considered a *drame bourgeois*, appearing some two decades before the genre was defined by Diderot. Two years after the death of Marivaux, Voltaire had *Le Mère confidente* in mind when he wrote ironically, "Il n'y a plus que les drames bourgeois du néologue Marivaux où l'on puisse pleurer en sûreté de conscience."[2] Of course, Voltaire himself dabbled in the genre of the tearful tragicomedy, and his sarcasm notwithstanding, *La Mère confidente* was well received, even though, initially, the *moliéresque* influence was not detected. The play had nineteen consecutive performances, and the *Mercure de France* remarked that *"La Mère confidente . . . est très-goûtée et très-suivie,"*[3] and shortly thereafter elaborated: "[The play] fut généralement applaudie par le mérite du Dialogue et par le jeu des Acteurs; elle fait un extrême plaisir, et attire beaucoup de monde à l'Hôtel de Bourgogne."[4] Other eighteenth-century critics, notably Desboulmiers[5] and Abbé La Porte, usually inimical to Marivaux, found certain modest qualities in *La Mère confidente*.[6] Most subsequent reviewers, however, either ignored it or stated their reservations concerning its merits. Claude Roy's assertion that *"La Mère confidente* c'est le seule bonne comédie de Diderot"[7] summarizes, in fact, the kind of interest most literary historians have shown in the play. Even E. J. H. Greene noted: "Even if one grants that *La Mère confidente* is the best *drame bourgeois* ever written, such academic generosity is not enough to make it a good play. In saying

---

[1]McKee, *Theater of Marivaux*, 182.
[2]See his June 1765 letter to the Marquis de Villette in Voltaire's *Correspondence*, 2, 385.
[3]*Le Mercure de France* (Paris), May 1735, p. 990.
[4]See the June 1735 issue, pp. 1187-1195.
[5]Desboulmiers, *Histoire anecdotique et raisonnée*, 4, 140-141.
[6]Porte, *L'Observateur littéraire*, 1, 95.
[7]Claude Roy, *Lire Marivaux* (Paris: Editions du Seuil, 1947), 79.

this, one parts company with Marivaux himself, for it was one of his seven favourites."[8]

The plot is somewhat akin to that of *L'Ecole des mères*, with this difference: the mother, instead of being overtly tyrannical, gives her daughter, Angélique, a certain amount of freedom. Two men aspire to her hand: Dorante, whom she has met in a park; a young man who is penniless and whose uncle, extremely rich but unashamedly young, cannot be expected to die soon; and Ergaste, the uncle, an individual who is too morose, too melancholic, and too sad for Angélique's taste. Madame Argante, the mother, opts for Ergaste, but does so more tactfully and while displaying a strategic measure of tender loving care corroborated by appropriate tears. To make sure that she is obeyed, however, she asks her daughter to take her into her confidence; to make extra sure, she has Lubin, a valet, spy on her behalf. Step by step she wins Angélique to her side. Later she disguises herself as her daughter's aunt in order to meet Dorante and reject him, but she is taken in by his charm and sincerity; with the help of Ergaste's understanding and ultimate capitulation, she finally is able to agree to the marriage of the two lovers and provide for the happy ending of the comedy.

The relationship between *La Mère confidente* and *L'Ecole des femmes* has been seen, so far, only by Emile Gossot. In speaking of *L'Ecole des mères* and *La Mère confidente* concomitantly, he declared: "Il me semble que ces deux comédies eussent gagné à être réuniës en une seule, comme l'a fait Molière pour *L'Ecole des femmes*, que Marivaux a prise pour modèle. On aurait eu ainsi l'exemple à côté de la leçon et l'effet cherché eut été plus immédiat et plus sûr."[9] Being concerned only with the moralist in Marivaux, Emile Gossot does not discuss at all the influence he perceives, nor does he state what the lesson and the effect might be. Perhaps these lacunae can be filled in the following paragraphs.

The scene in which Arnolphe asks Agnès to break with her lover is probably the source for I, 8 in Marivaux's comedy in which Madame Argante makes a similar request, even though she treats Angélique less drastically and with more apparent good will. At the same time, Arnolphe had demanded simply and straightforwardly:

Et quant au monsieur là, je prétends, s'il vous plaît,
Dût le mettre au tombeau le mal dont il vous berce,
Qu'avec lui vous rompiez désormais tout commerce;
Que, venant au logis pour votre compliment,
Vous lui fermiez au nez la porte honnêtement;

[8]Greene, *Marivaux*, 196.
[9]Emile Gossot, *Marivaux moraliste* (Paris: Didier, 1881), 48-49.

Et lui jetant, s'il heurte, un grès par la fenêtre,
L'obligiez tout de bon à ne plus y paraître. (III, 1)

Marivaux's mother, more hypocritically and less comically, engages in the following bit of dialogue with her daughter.

MADAME ARGANTE: . . . l'as-tu vu souvent?

ANGELIQUE: Dix ou douze fois.

MADAME ARGANTE: Le verras-tu encore?

ANGELIQUE: Franchement, j'aurai bien de la peine à m'en empêcher.

MADAME ARGANTE: Je t'offre, si tu le veux, de reprendre ma qualité de mère pour te le défendre. (I, 8)

Another instance of similarity between Molière's play and that of Marivaux emerges from a comparison between the scenes in which Arnolphe and Madame Argante express their despair and dismay concerning the unexpected results of the strict upbringing they had undertaken. However, once more Arnolphe's admonition is more to the point.

Quoi! j'aurai dirigé son éducation
Avec tant de tendresse et de précaution;
Je l'aurai fait passer chez moi dès son enfance,
Et j'en aurai chéri la plus tendre espérance . . .
Afin qu'un jeune fou dont elle s'amourache,
Me la vint enlever jusque sur la moustache. (IV, 1)

Madame Argante's complaint, on the other hand, is essentially the same: "Hélas! ma fille, vois ce que tu as fait; te serais-tu cru capable de tromper ta mère, de voir à son insu un jeune étourdi, de courir les risques de son indiscrétion et de sa vanité, de t'exposer à tout ce qu'il voudra dire, et de te livrer à l'indécence de tant d'entrevues secrètes" (I, 8). Thus, both Madame Argante and Arnolphe have brought up a young girl, have cared for her, have educated her, and have made the necessary arrangements for her marriage; both now are faced with the young girl's love for someone else, with their being disappointed in their expectations and fooled in their trust all because of a *jeune fou* in Molière's play and a *jeune étourdi* in Marivaux's comedy.

The second act of *La Mère confidente* also contains two situations reminiscent of Molière's *L'Ecole des femmes*. Certain parts of the celebrated letter Agnès wrote to Horace need to be cited here: "On me dit fort que tous les jeunes hommes sont des trompeurs, qu'il ne les faut point écouter, et que tout ce que vous me dites n'est que pour m'abuser; mais je vous assure que je n'ai pu encore me figurer cela de vous, et je suis si touchée de vos paroles, que je ne saurais croire qu'elles soient menteuses" (III, 4). Similarly, Angélique states her apprehensions concerning young men in a speech she addresses to Dorante: "Si

Monsieur, comme je l'ai déjà dit, et à l'exemple de presque tous les
jeunes gens, était homme à faire trophée d'une aventure dont je suis
tout à fait innocente, où en serais-je?" (II, 3); and later in the same act,
still speaking to her lover, she reaffirms her fears only to try to persuade
herself, like Agnès, that they are groundless: "Excusez . . . l'embarras
où se trouve une fille de mon âge, timide et vertueuse; il y a tant de
pièges dans la vie! j'ai si peu d'expérience! serait-il si difficile de me
tromper si on voulait? Je n'ai que ma sagesse et mon innocence pour
toute ressource, et quand on n'a que cela, on peut avoir peur; mais me
voilà bien rassurée" (II, 6). Thus, both Angélique and Agnès, inspired
by Madame Argante and Arnolphe, respectively, question their lover in
strikingly similar terms. And in both cases, love prevails, and they are
able to rely on the reassurance that sentiments supply.

Another example of a probable Molière-inspired situation occurs in
La Mère confidente when Angélique, who confides to her mother
throughout the play, moves the latter to remark: "*à part les premiers
mots:* Sa franchise me pénètre" (III, 8). These words recall Arnolphe's
pitiful observation, "Cet aveu qu'elle fait avec sincérité / Me marque
pour le moins son ingénuité" (II, 6). The situation is the same: Agnès
causes Arnolphe's remark after she confesses to him that, contrary to
his instructions, she allowed Horace to visit with her; Angélique, too,
occasions Madame Argante's remark when she admits to her that she
continues to see Dorante despite the orders received. Moreover, both
authors give similar instructions to the actors for the lines in question:
Madame Argante's stage indications have been quoted above; those
that Molière gives to the actor playing the role of Arholphe are, for the
speech in question, *bas, à part*.

In addition, as was the case in the comparison between *L'Ecole des
femmes* and *L'Ecole des mères*, resemblances may be seen often in the
instances of revolt and of submission practiced by Agnès and
Angélique. Similarities are present throughout *La Mère confidente*, and
space limitations preclude their inclusion here. Suffice it to point out,
though, that Angélique's mutiny is always less emphatic, and her
obedience more constant than the defiance and yielding episodes in
which her predecessor engages.

Another parallel that should be pointed out between the two plays is
constituted by the relationship of Arnolphe to Horace and that of
Ergaste to Dorante. In *L'Ecole des femmes*, Horace fails to connect the
constant presence of Arnolphe near Agnès' house with the rival Agnès
had cautioned him about. Throughout the play he finds it impossible
not to chat with Arnolphe about his love for Agnès and about his plans.
Likewise, in *La Mère confidente*, Dorante meets with his uncle and
rival, Ergaste, and is ingenuous enough to confess his love for

Angélique. And like Arnolphe, Dorante does not associate the presence of Ergaste near the house of Madame Argante with the rival of whom both Angélique and her maid, Lisette, had spoken previously. Thus, Dorante and Horace share in a certain amount of inexperience, and they manifest it in exactly the same fashion. It should be recalled, also, that Ergaste, like Arnolphe, cedes in favor of the younger man, although the capitulation of the former is more voluntary than that of the latter.

The rapports between *La Mère confidente* and *L'Ecole des femmes* are such that they appear to corroborate Emile Gossot's statement quoted earlier. Yet, as in the case of previously discussed plays, Marivaux departs to some extent from the *moliéresque* model. Such departure has been alluded to already when mention was made of the differences between the acts of revolt and of submission of the respective heroines. There is more. Madame Argante, for example, unlike Arnolphe in his efforts with Agnès, does not bring up her daughter with the intention of making her totally ignorant. The education that she administers leaves mother and daughter with the possibility of communication and reciprocating tenderness. Of course, this feeling is impaired when Madame Argante slyly persuades Angélique to confess everything to her, and also when she decides to have Lubin spy on the comings and goings of Angélique. These acts, however, do not deteriorate into the entirely inimical relationship that develops between Arnolphe and Agnès in Molière's play. Another difference emerges from a comparison between the more tempestuous Agnès and the more placid Angélique. Molière's heroine writes to her lover, sees him repeatedly, and even suggests to him that they elope, but Angélique, on her part, almost always hesitates, at times refuses to meet Dorante, and does not wish even to consider the idea of eloping, an idea that orginates, in Marivaux's reworking of the theme, with Dorante. In fact, unlike her predecessor, who always took the initiative, Angélique needs her Lisette to such an extent that the maid has no choice but to assume the role of a temptress in order not to have her mistress submit entirely to the wishes of Madame Argante. Moreover, the difference in tone between the two plays is obvious throughout. Molière's is highly comical, often cruel, almost always imperious; whereas Marivaux's is affectionate, compassionate, and almost committed, as if the author purposefully wanted to point out the proper relationship between mother and daughter. This, of course, is rightfully a tone to be chosen by a playwright of a *drame bourgeois*, but, as Petit de Julleville put it, the effort still resulted in "un petit chef-d'oeuvre dans un genre un peu bâtard."[10]

---

[10]Petit de Julleville, *Le Théâtre en France* (Paris: Nouvelle Edition, 1923), 277.

Perhaps what spoiled it all for *La Mère confidente* is the fact that Angélique, even more than the Angélique of *L'Ecole des mères*, fails to impress readers and spectators as a true-to-life character. Unlike Agnès, whose words and deeds are immediately understandable because they are logical and constitute the expected effect of her particular circumstances, the heroine of *La Mère confidente* speaks and acts in retrogressive fashion, in ways that one has come to consider abolished since the creation of the unforgettable Agnès. Her agreement, for example, to tell her love secrets to her mother is totally unbelievable, even if one admits that Angélique is dominated by Madame Argante; at any rate, the episode is devoid of psychological truth. Larroumet suggested this in his discussion of the play: "Mais, dira-t-on, Mme Argante trompe sa fille; elle apporte une arrière-pensée dans ce rôle de franchise et d'abandon réciproque; la mère ne saurait ignorer ce que la confidente apprendra et ne pas en profiter. . . . La confidente d'une jeune fille ne peut guère recevoir que des confidences d'amour; aussi, dans une scène exquise de délicatesse, Angélique raconte-t-elle bientôt son aventure avec Dorante."[11] But the critic did not elaborate by pointing directly to the dramatist's error. The exquisiteness and the delicateness that he mentions do not convey credibility to the scene. Angélique's confession to her mother does not have any of the ingredients that made Agnès' admissions to Arnolphe entirely to the point and believable. Agnès told everything, or almost, because no one ever instructed her that what she did was wrong (or, perhaps, because she took advantage of such lack of instruction while being able to distinguish right from wrong in matters of love and courtship, and the admissions constituted a chance of punishing Arnolphe). On the contrary, Angélique's confession is tainted by tenderness and sentimentality, aspects that lend to it the questionable aura of soap opera. Moreover, Angélique should have known better, and one expected her to know better. In the scene in which Madame Argante makes her request to become the daughter's confidante, she met indeed with resistance.

MADAME ARGANTE: Te rappelles-tu, chère Antélique, le sujet de l'entretien que
    nous eûmes l'autre jour, et cette douceur que nous nous figurions toutes
    deux à vivre ensemble dans la plus intime confiance, sans avoir de secrets
    l'une pour l'autre; t'en souviens-tu? Nous fûmes interrompues; et comme
    cette idée-là te réjouit beaucoup, exécutons-la; parle-moi à coeur ouvert;
    fais-moi ta confidente.

ANGELIQUE: Vous, la confidente de votre fille?

[11] Larroumet, *Marivaux, sa vie et ses oeuvres,* 279.

MADAME ARGANTE: Oh! votre fille! Eh! qui te parle d'elle? Ce n'est point ta mère qui veut être ta confidente; c'est ton amie, encore une fois.

ANGELIQUE, *riant:* D'accord, mais mon amie redira tout à ma mère, l'une est inséparable de l'autre.

MADAME ARGANTE: Eh bien! je les sépare, moi; je t'en fais serment. Oui, mets-toi dans l'esprit que ce que tu me confieras sur ce pied-là, c'est comme si ta mère ne l'entendait pas. Eh! mais cela se doit; il y aurait mauvaise foi à faire autrement. (I, 2)

Her initial opposition notwithstanding, Angélique in Scene 8 of the same act, does exactly what her mother requested. This contradicts the expectation of readers and spectators, and Angélique appears to be no more than wax manipulated by Madame Argante's fingers, much as Arnolphe had tried, but unsuccessfully, to treat Agnès. One almost feels like standing up and telling Angélique that she is supposed to be the enlightened *jeune fille* of the eighteenth century who should have learned by heart the example of Molière's heroine, rather than retrogress to a state of filial obedience, which gives a shot in the arm, once more, to parental totalitarianism.

Little wonder that, after its eighteenth-century run, *La Mère confidente*, disappeared from the theatrical repertory for a long time; and when it was presented once more in 1863, it caused the romantic Sainte-Beuve to remark about Marivaux: "Dans *La Mère confidente*, qui sort de ses données habituelles et qui est d'un ordre à part dans son théâtre, il a touché des cordes plus franches, plus sensibles et d'une nature meilleure."[12] On the other hand, the more lucid Théophile Gautier noted, "N'est-ce pas une chose utile que de montrer les côtés par où pèchent ces grands écrivains qu'on admire?"[13] Apparently Gautier saw the psychological lapses in *La Mère confidente*. The unnaturalness of a daughter confiding her amorous secrets to her mother is only one example of such a lapse. One could cite several more: the depiction of a tender, sympathetic, and extremely loving Madame Argante, who, nevertheless, employs a servant to spy on Angélique (although Arnolphe had used the services of a spy also, his action was understandable, in fact anticipated, because he was moved only by his egotism); the description of an allegedly superior maternal behavior that, nevertheless, uses such dubious and devious means as approaching a daughter's suitor under the disguise of an aunt, while all the time preaching to the daughter on the usefulness of truth and other virtues; the capitulation of Ergaste, a capitulation that is unacceptable both because he is not the usual old and sour uncle who is pushed into a

---

[12]C. A. Sainte-Beuve, *Causeries du lundi* (Paris: Garnier, n.d.), 9, 376.
[13]Théophile Gautier, *Le Moniteur universel* (Paris), 28 September 1863, p. 5.

corner at the end of the play and has no choice but to give up, and because, prior to Act III, he had been drawn as an unintelligent, uncourteous individual in whose case one could not foresee such gallant acts as giving up Angélique and his wealth for the benefit of another man. "The play is false from beginning to end,"[14] concluded one of the most constant admirers of Marivaux. And in the words of another, it is only "a sad piece of false sentimentality."[15]

The initial success of *La Mère confidente*, then, can be explained only in terms of the newness of the idea of a daughter, placed in the higher levels of society, who confides to her mother. Although psychologically weak, the novelty of the idea must have been startling. However, once the general demise of the *drame bourgeois* occurred, *La Mère confidente* became a museum piece, and its *moliéresque* episodes, reworked and misapplied to characters of another century, failed to supply Marivaux with the support he needed to have his dramatic effort survive.

[14]Greene, *Marivaux*, 198.
[15]Mandel, *Seven Comedies by Marivaux*, 11.

LES FAUSSES CONFIDENCES

Hardly anyone has said anything derogatory about *Les Fausses confidences*, and most critics have agreed that it is impossible to determine whether it or *Le Jeu de l'amour et du hasard* is the true masterpiece in Marivaux's theatrical repertory. Although when it was first presented in 1737 it had only a mediocre success,[1] the play has sustained an almost uninterrupted popularity in France, and after World War II it was the calling card of the Jean-Louis Barrault Company, which carried it to the four quarters of the globe. That *Les Fausses confidences* is among Marivaux's best plays, that it is one of his most characteristic, one of the most likely to survive for centuries to come, and one most worthy of survival are not debatable points, and they would not be stressed here were it not for the fact that the *moliéresque* influence is nevertheless present even in one of his most acclaimed comedies. A few excerpts of such acclaim appear, then, in order, for if it can be established that Marivaux relied to an appreciable extent on Molière even in his most original and typical effort, then D'Alembert's report on the playwright's dislike of the seventeenth-century master may be considered false (either because D'Alembert misinterpreted Marivaux on this subject, or because Marivaux did not express his true feelings to his friend).

Marcel Arland, for example, stated unequivocally that "il n'a rien écrit d'aussi vif, d'aussi personnel, ni d'aussi proche de la perfection que . . . *les Fausses Confidences*."[2] Kenneth N. McKee was equally complimentary: "Marivaux was at the peak of his career. . . . His creative power was at its height. In such an aura of literary effulgence Marivaux composed *Les Fausses confidences*. . . . It occupies a place of pre-eminent importance in Marivaux's theater, and its popularity in the twentieth century bids fair to make it with *Le Jeu* as his most highly regarded work."[3] And at the end of his chapter on the play he concluded, "*Les Fausses confidences* emerges as one of the very fine plays of the classical theater in France."[4] For his part, E. J. H. Greene confirmed: "Today it [*Les Fausses confidences*] is firmly established as a classic: it has a long history of stage production behind it . . . it

---

[1] See J. E. Gueullette's comments in *Notes et souvenirs sur le Théâtre-Italien au XVIII siècle* (Paris: E. Droz, 1938), 123; also *Le Mercure de France* (Paris), July 1738, p. 1620; and Simon-Henri Dubuisson, *Lettres du Commissaire Dubuisson au Marquis de Caumont* (Paris: P. Arnould, 1882), letter dated 1 April 1737.

[2] Arland, *Marivaux*, 99.

[3] McKee, *Theater of Marivaux*, 202.

[4] *Ibid.*, 219.

has . . . acquired a body of serious critical comment."[5] And then he
went on to conclude that "it is idle to ask whether *Les Fausses
confidences* is a better play than *Le Jeu,* or most characteristic of its
author; both are masterpieces."[6] However, admiration of the play not
only was stated formally by admirers of Marivaux, it was confirmed also
by reviewers for newspapers and magazines who reiterated consistently
the popular acceptance of *Les Fausses confidences.*[7]

The question that now arises is: Is Marivaux free from the influence
of Molière, that is, is this, perhaps his best dramatic endeavor, composed without any reference, voluntary or not, to the plays of Molière?
Speaking of *Les Fausses confidences,* some critics settle the question
with no hesitation: "Tous les auteurs qui, à diverses réprises, ont rendu
à la comédie française son éclat, sa valeur morale, sa force
d'expansion, se réclament hautement de lui [de Molière]."[8] This type
of reasoning, however, is erroneous because it tends to prove that any
good author of comedies is a disciple of Molière. Yet, although
Marivaux specialists have pointed to other sources of influence for *Les
Fausses confidences,*[9] they have said nothing about the *moliéresque*
traces that persist here and there in measurable fashion. On the other
hand, the critics of Molière, less expert on Marivaux but also less aware
of words or sentiments attributed to Marivaux in regard to the
seventeenth-century dramatist, have not failed to see a relationship
between *Les Fausses confidences* and some of Molière's dramatic out-
put. Once again we find, therefore, Molière specialists commenting on
the sources of Marivaux. Emile Fabre declared: "Marivaux . . . reprit
cependant le thème [he is referring to *La Princesse d'Elide*] de son
prédécesseur: dans *Les Fausses confidences* . . . il mit aussi en
présence des amoureux et dans chaque couple, tantôt la femme, tantôt
l'homme, qui se donnent le singulier plaisir d'alarmer et de faire
pleurer l'amant ou l'amante pour s'assurer de son obéissance et du don
total de sa personne."[10] Maurice Donnay pointed to similarities
between *Les Fausses confidences* and another play by Molière, *Les
Amants magnifiques:* "L'on voit que, par sa colère, son dépit, sa
pudeur, sa curiosité, la fière et tendre Eriphile [heroine of *Les Amants
magnifiques*] est, elle aussi, une ancêtre des héroïnes de Marivaux.
Elle deviendra l'Araminte des *Fausses confidences*";[11] and then he

---

[5]Greene, *Marivaux,* 208.
[6]*Ibid.,* 217.
[7]For a summary of such critical opinion see McKee, *Theater of Marivaux,* 212-218.
[8]Lafenestre, *Molière,* 193.
[9]More about which later.
[10]Emile Fabre, *Molière* (Paris: Gallimard, 1928), 194.
[11]Donnay, *Molière,* 309.

added the following clear-cut conclusion: "Marivaux voulait s'éloigner de Molière: il s'en éloignait comme une rivière s'éloigne de sa source."[12] Georges Lafenestre agreed with Maurice Donnay with regard to *Les Amants magnifiques* being, in part, the source of *Les Fausses confidences:* "Marivaux, au théâtre, cherche son inspiration dans les oeuvres oubliées qu'on ne lit guère. *Les Amants magnifiques* deviennent *Les Fausses confidences*."[13] It should be pointed out at the outset, however, that these statements are not supported by examples. Normally, lack of textual comparisons would suffice to raise one's suspicions. Yet, as has been shown in a number of previous chapters, Molière did state a theme in *La Princesse d'Elide* that Marivaux repeatedly reorchestrated in several of his plays. And, insofar as *Les Amants magnifiques* is concerned, textual comparisons do indeed reveal the *moliéresque* background.

It will be recalled that the plot of *Les Fausses confidences* deals with the old problem of the feasibility of marriage between two persons who occupy, financially, a very different position in society. Dorante, a penniless man, loves Araminte, a rich widow, in whose employ he enters. Araminte, who is courted by the Count, becomes aware of Dorante's sentiments through the devices of Dubois (who tells Araminte that his master has a mental illness that is the result of his passion for her; who arranges for a box containing Araminte's portrait to be discovered by the latter, and so forth) and, after due surprises and numerous adventures, she is prompted to reciprocate Dorante's love.

"De quelle émotion sens-je mon coeur atteint?" (IV, 4), a line that Marivaux had used by altering it on a number of previous occasions, recalls the sentiments of Araminte's "Il me touche tant, qu'il faut que je m'en aille" (II, 2), which reflects faithfully the sentiments of Molière's Princess.

In the episode of the portrait, Dubois' implication that Dorante might be in love with Marton, *suivante* of Araminte, awakens spite in the latter and crystallizes the birth of love for Dorante, just as Euryale's implication that he might be in love with Aglante, cousin of the Princess, causes the latter to have no more doubts as to the object of her sentiments. Another instance of similarity emerges from the fact that Moron, while appearing to defend the interests of the Princess, actually contrives with Euryale to subdue her; likewise, Dubois plots with Dorante against Araminte, his mistress, by using the devices described above. It should be pointed out, however, that Moron's efforts are less

[12]*Ibid.*, 309.
[13]Lafenestre, *Molière*, 192.

strenuous and less comic than the unscrupulous antics in which Dubois engages.

Although it is true that many heroines are apt to be spited into love; that the strategy utilized by Moron and Dubois is not uncommon; that servants who cannot be trusted are numerous in dramatic literature, Araminte's and the Princess' sentiments are equally abrupt when they realize that they are in love; the plots of Dubois and Moron are immediately fruitful; finally, both Moron and Dubois fool their respective mistresses in a similar manner. To this extent — and not a meager one — *Les Fausses confidences* has been influenced by *La Princesse d'Elide*. Nevertheless Marivaux's originality can be seen from the way he departed from the first *surprise de l'amour:* although the Princess does not know that Euryale loves her until the very end of the play, Araminte is informed of Dorante's love as soon as the curtain rises; the Princess has an aversion to marriage, and the surprises, the *dépits* she experiences, are destined to eliminate this aversion, although Araminte contemplates marrying the Count, and Dorante has to face the problem of a rival *en chair et en os;* finally, the Princess is young and childish, Araminte is mature, understanding, and strong in her protection of Dorante, in her contradiction of her mother, who does not agree with her sentiments for Dorante, and in her expression of an uncommon desire to marry an employee.

The similarities between *Les Fausses confidences* and *Les Amants magnifiques* are, however, more specific. At the rise of the curtain, Molière's hero, Sostrate, who loves the princess Eriphile, discusses his misfortunes with Clitidas, the valet.

> CLITIDAS: Allez, allez, vous vous moquez; un peu de hardiesse réussit toujours aux amants . . .
>
> SOSTRATE: Trop de choses, hélas! condamnent mes feux à un éternel silence.
>
> CLITIDAS: Et quoi?
>
> SOSTRATE: La bassesse de ma fortune . . . qui met entre elle et mes désirs une distance si fâcheuse.
>
> CLITIDAS: Ma conjecture est fondée . . . et je veux éclaircir un peu cette petite affaire-là. . . . Laissez-moi faire, je suis de vos amis; les gens de mérite me touchent, et je veux prendre mon temps pour entretenir la princesse. (I, 1)

Likewise, in Marivaux's play, Dorante informs Dubois, who is in the service of Araminte, of his futile love for the latter and of his despair of not being able to marry a richer woman than he; whereupon the following discussion ensues.

> DUBOIS: Tenez, en un mot, je suis content de vous; vous m'avez toujours plu; vous êtes un excellent homme, un homme que j'aime.
>
> DORANTE: Cette femme-ci [Araminte] a un rang dans le monde . . . et tu crois

qu'elle fera quelque attention à moi, que je l'épouserai, moi qui ne suis rien, moi qui n'ai point de bien?

DUBOIS: Eh! que diantre! un peu de confiance; vous réussirez, vous dis-je. Je m'en charge. (I, 2)

In both scenes, then, a poor man is in love with a rich woman of considerable social status; this is not uncommon in dramatic literature, nor is the fact that a servant attempts to encourage the poor man and to work on his behalf. But it is uncommon for this servant to be in the service of the woman loved and to contrive with the poor pretender behind the mistress' back. It is also worthy of note that Clitidas' *un peu de hardiesse réussit toujours aux amants* corresponds to Dubois' *un peu de confiance; vous réussirez;* that Sostrate's complaint in the phrase *la bassesse de ma fortune* becomes *moi qui n'ai pas de bien* in the mouth of Dorante; that Clitidas' *je suis de vos amis; les gens de mérite me touchent* is echoed by Dubois' *je suis content de vous; vous m'avez toujours plu; vous êtes un excellent homme, un homme que j'aime;* finally that *Ma conjecture est fondée* of Molière's personage is changed only slightly by Marivaux in Dubois' *je m'en charge.*

Another resemblance may be observed in the *fausses confidences* that Clitidas uses to engage Eriphile on behalf of Sostrate.

CLITIDAS: Il [Sostrate] a quelque chose dans la tête . . . Il . . . m'a parlé de votre personne avec des transports les plus grands du monde, vous a mise au-dessus du ciel, et vous a donné toutes les louanges qu'on peut donner à la princesse la plus accomplie de la terre, entremêlant tout cela de soupirs qui disaient plus qu'il ne voulait. Enfin, à force de le tourner de tous côtés, et de le presser sur la cause de cette mélancolie dont toute la cour s'aperçoit, il a été contraint de m'avouer qu'il était amoureux.

ERIPHILE: Comment, amoureux! quelle témérité est la sienne! c'est un extravagant que je ne verrais de ma vie.

CLITIDAS: Il faut vous dire la vérité. J'ai tiré de son coeur, par surprise, un secret qu'il veut cacher à tout le monde, et avec lequel il est, dit-il, résolu de mourir. Il a été au désespoir du vol subtil que je lui en ai fait; et, bien loin de me charger de vous le découvrir, il m'a conjuré, avec toutes les instantes prières qu'on saurait faire, de ne vous en rien révéler; et c'est trahison contre lui que ce que je viens de vous dire. (II, 3)

Likewise, Dubois uses the *confidences* of his predecessor in a scene that is altogether quite similar to the one previously quoted:

DUBOIS: Son [Dorante's] défaut est là. *Il se touche le front.* C'est à la tête que le mal le tient.

ARAMINTE: A la tête?

DUBOIS: Oui . . . il y a six mois qu'il est tombé fou; il y a six mois qu'il extravague d'amour, qu'il en a la cervelle brûlée, qu'il en est comme un perdu.

ARAMINTE: Il fera ce qu'il voudra, mais je ne le garderai pas . . . je veux le congédier.

DUBOIS: Il ne vous dira mot [about his love for her]; jamais vous n'entendrez parler de son amour.

ARAMINTE: En est-tu bien sûr?

DUBOIS: Oh! il ne faut pas en avoir peur; il mourrait plutôt. (I, 14)

Like Clitidas, Dubois starts out by intimating that Dorante is demented in some way; like Clitidas, then, Dubois explains that Dorante's behavior is caused by his extreme love. Both Eriphile and Araminte interrupt the *confidences* made with harsh words of not seeing (in Molière's play) and of discharging (in Marivaux's) their respective lover; whereupon both servants declare that their *confidences* have been made without the consent of the lover, who wishes to preserve the secret: Sostrate being *résolu de mourir* with it, whereas Dorante, rather than affirming it, *mourrait plutôt*. The similarities of situation, tone, and vocabulary cannot be merely coincidental. And, although I, 2 and I, 14 are the only scenes in Marivaux's comedy that bear a direct resemblance to the plays of Molière, these are scenes of key importance in *Les Fausses confidences*.

Elsewhere, there are a number of differences between Marivaux's comedy and those of Molière to which it has been compared. The way in which the dramatist departed from the theme furnished by *La Princesse d'Elide* has been discussed. The manner in which he alters the data of *Les Amants magnifiques* is equally visible. Eriphile, for example, is young, easily angered, proud; Araminte is mature, more understanding, modest. Aristione, mother of Eriphile, is not so headstrong as Madame Argante, mother of Araminte, who disapproves of Dorante throughout the play. There is also a notable difference between the impetuous rivals of Sostrate, Iphicrate and Timocles, and the peaceful and forgiving Count, rival of Dorante.

Understandably, just as the critics of Marivaux usually are prone to diminish the importance of the *moliéresque* influence, so, too, Molière specialists remain inclined at times to give it unwarranted proportions. It is interesting to observe that Petitot, who annotated part of the Molière edition published by Charles Louandres, declared: "Cette scène [Act II, Scene 3] et la suivante sont le premier modèle du genre de Marivaux, dont presque toutes les pièces roulent sur cette idée. Mais combien n'a-t-on pas abusé des petites nuances et des raffinements que ce genre semble exiger!"[14] There is a marked contrast between a comment of this type, which summarizes some of the miscon-

---

[14]See p. 000.

ceptions of Molière specialists who see in Marivaux only a poor imitator, and equally debatable affirmations of admirers of the eighteenth-century playwright who, unmindful of valid comparisons, state, as Kenneth N. McKee does, "*Les Fausses confidences*, distinctly original for its day, was without tangible sources,"[15] an uncorroborated assumption repeated with equal dispatch by E. J. H. Greene at the beginning of his chapter on the play, "Once again the search for sources has turned up nothing."[16]

Molière experts, for whom often any other comedy writer appears presumptuous and worthy of haughty neglect, are impressed only by the shortcomings of the practice of *marivaudage* and fail to comment on its value relating to the depiction of delicate nuances and shades of feelings that add to a spectator's total appreciation of a dramatic effort. These experts do not acknowledge that the stifled and dry prose and versification of many of Marivaux's contemporaries appear unworthy indeed of comparison with the frequent freshness and refinement that one finds at times in the theater of Marivaux (especially in *Les Fausses confidences*). *Aficionados* of his theater, on the other hand, in a vain effort to eliminate whatever *moliéresque* recollections are present, follow either the procedure of pointing to remote sources in the theater of others, or of attributing to Marivaux innovations that are difficult to defend. In the case of *Les Fausses confidences*, as in the case of so many other plays before it, critics have mentioned again Lope de Vega's *Le Chien du jardinier:* Hippolyte Lucas and Xavier de Courville, for example, saw certain similarities that, however, they did not specify,[17] and that, after close perusal of the texts, remain mysterious. Jean Fleury mentioned, but without the necessary elaboration or specificity, the possible influence of Lafont's *L'Amour vengé*.[18] The only connection, and a remote one it is, resides in the fact that in *L'Amour vengé* two people fall in love after being told, separately, that each loves the other; in Marivaux's play, however, only one person is so told, the other, Dorante, being in love with Araminte from the very beginning of the comedy. E. J. H. Greene dedicated one brief sentence to a little-known play of Riccoboni, *La Dame amoureuse par envie*, and to an equally unknown story by Robert Charles, *Histoire de Dupuis et de Mme de Londé*.[19] But he concluded that the memories only could have been involuntary and are not worth going into. This is true, of course, but the

[15]McKee, *Theater of Marivaux*, 209.

[16]Greene, *Marivaux*, 208.

[17]See Hippolyte Lucas, *Histoire du Théâtre-Français* (Paris: Charles Gosselin, 1843), 1, 335; and Courville, *Luigi Riccoboni dit Lélio*, 1, 65.

[18]Fleury, *Marivaux et le marivaudage*, 138.

[19]Greene, *Marivaux*, 208.

mere mention of distant and unspecified sources does not obliterate the
very real *moliéresque* recollections. Nor does the other favorite procedure of praising in the theater of Marivaux certain questionable *firsts*.
When Kenneth N. McKee, for example, declares that "this is the first
play in the French theater that ends by a marriage which cuts across
social lines,"[20] he forgets that *Les Amants magnifiques* does so to an
even greater degree: Sostrate is only a general, whereas Eriphile is a
princess; but both Dorante and Araminte belong to the bourgeosie, the
difference between them being solely a monetary one.

Marivaux's originality in *Les Fausses confidences* need not be sought
elsewhere than in his treatment of the heroine, and in his particular
style. Araminte is described by a dramatist who obviously is kinder to
women than Molière and any of his followers at the beginning of the
eighteenth century. She is gentle, modest, yet curious, even inquisi-
tive; but above all, she is naturally inclined to forgive (even when she is
being taken advantage of by Dubois' and Dorante's lies) and to love with
disarming ingenuity. She is totally above pretense and coquetry, and
her good nature allows her to display, at the same time, both an overt
consideration for others and an unobtrusive, quiet air of authority that
enhances her feminine dignity and charm. Araminte's poise is particularly noticeable when she finds herself in the middle, between a
somewhat arrogant and domineering mother in the person of Madame
Argante, and a handsome, intriguing, but calculating Dorante. In such
a situation she neither falters nor retains any rancor. Instead, she is
able to spread her own better disposition to the others by the utterance
of a kind word or by an unexpected gesture of understanding, or love,
which catches the others by surprise and bestows an aura of serenity on
the entire scene. There is very little of the spiteful Princesse d'Elide or
of the youthful, anger-prone Eriphile in Marivaux's character. In fact,
Araminte is perhaps one of the sweetest, most ingratiating women in the
French theater, and she comes very close to being the ideal one: a
person who is likeable because she ultimately brings out the best in
those around her. Paul Gazagne, whose concern for the flesh and blood
of Marivaux's heroines is a steady one, looked upon Araminte's quick
acceptance of Dorante not in terms of the playwright's wish to conform
to the unity of time, rather as proof of the character's desire to turn once
more to an active sexual life following the loss of her husband.[21] E. J. H.
Greene chided Gazagne in this context, "Araminte never climbed onto
a streetcar named Desire,"[22] and indicated that if she had, her person-

[20]McKee, *Theater of Marivaux*, 209.
[21]Gazagne, *Marivaux par lui-même*, 112-115.
[22]Greene, *Marivaux*, 213.

ality would have been diminished. But he did not explain why a woman who rides on such a streetcar is necessarily less worthy of admiration. After all, at no time is Araminte guilty of saying, acting, or even feeling anything that would be in contradiction with her own deep sensitivity for what is logical and right. Streetcars named Desire might well be ridden, and more often, by persons such as Araminte, especially for the benefit of others, and Gazagne's depiction does not detract from the universal esteem in which Marivaux's heroine is held.

The playwright's stylistic originality is apparent, of course, in many scenes of *Les Fausses confidences*. But his genius for wording the surprise of love by dotting it with just the right amount of hesitations, naïveté, and expressions of budding passion is perhaps nowhere more apparent than in the delicately balanced dialogue of Act III, Scene 12 between Araminte and Dorante:

ARAMINTE: Approchez, Dorante.

DORANTE: Je n'ose presque paraître devant vous.

ARAMINTE, *à part:* Ah! je n'ai guère plus d'assurance que lui. *(Haut.)* Pourquoi vouloir me rendre compte de mes papiers? Je m'en fie bien à vous; ce n'est pas là-dessus que j'aurai à me plaindre.

DORANTE: Madame . . . j'ai autre chose à dire . . . je suis si interdit, si tremblant, que je ne saurais parler.

ARAMINTE, *à part, avec émotion:* Ah! que je crains la fin de tout ceci!

DORANTE, *ému:* Un de vos fermiers est venu tantôt, Madame.

ARAMINTE, *émue:* Un de mes fermiers? . . . cela se peut.

DORANTE: Oui, Madame . . . il est venu.

ARAMINTE, *toujours émue:* Je n'en doute pas.

DORANTE, *ému:* Et j'ai de l'argent à vous remettre.

ARAMINTE: Ah! de l'argent . . . nous verrons.

DORANTE: Quand il vous plaira, Madame, de le recevoir.

ARAMINTE: Oui . . . je le recevrai . . . vous me le donnerez. *(A part.)* Je ne sais ce que je lui réponds.

DORANTE: Ne serait-il pas temps de vous l'apporter ce soir ou demain, Madame?

ARAMINTE: Demain, dites-vous? Comment vous garder jusque-là, après ce qui est arrivé?

DORANTE, *plaintivement:* De tout le temps de ma vie que je vais passer loin de vous, je n'aurais plus que ce seul jour qui m'en serait précieux.

ARAMINTE: Il n'y a pas moyen, Dorante; il faut se quitter. On sait que vous m'aimez, et l'on croirait que je n'en suis pas fâchée.

DORANTE: Hélas! Madame, que je vais être à plaindre!

ARAMINTE: Ah! allez, Dorante, chacun a ses chagrins.

DORANTE: J'ai tout perdu! J'avais un portrait et je ne l'ai plus.

ARAMINTE: A quoi vous sert de l'avoir? Vous savez peindre.

DORANTE: Je ne pourrai de longtemps m'en dédommager; d'ailleurs, celui-ci m'aurait été bien cher! Il a été entre vos mains, Madame.

ARAMINTE: Mais vous n'êtes pas raisonnable.

DORANTE: Ah! Madame, je vais être éloigné de vous; vous serez assez vengée; n'ajoutez rien à ma douleur.

ARAMINTE: Vous donner mon portrait! Songez-vous que ce serait avouer que je vous aime?

DORANTE: Que vous m'aimez, Madame! Quelle idée! qui pourrait se l'imaginer?

ARAMINTE, *d'un ton vif et naïf:* Et voilà pourtant ce qui m'arrive. (III, 12)

There is very little that is *moliéresque* in the dialogue above, and none of it, or almost none could have been thought of or expressed more delicately by anyone else. Marivaux's inventiveness need not be looked for in his alleged dislike for Molière, nor in his alleged ability to compose without reference to the seventeenth-century master. His originality is sufficiently present in his heroine and especially in those scenes in which she appears.

LES SINCERES

Unlike the case of *Les Fausses confidences*, both Molière and Marivaux critics have associated *Les Sincères* with the heritage of the seventeenth-century playwright as it was left in the celebrated *Le Misanthrope*, which is clearly the source of Marivaux's play. The only subject for debate is, so far, the extent to which *Le Misanthrope* influenced the eighteenth-century dramatist.

It is interesting to note that, when *Les Sincères* was first presented on 13 January 1739 at the Théâtre Italien, the name of the author was withheld, and the audience expressed its pleasure with a great deal of ovation. The following night, the anonymity of the playwright vanished, and the comedy was booed by a suddenly unsympathetic, even violent public. No immediately valid explanation can be proposed for this switch in reaction, but one wonders if a reworking of such a well-known play as *Le Misanthrope* might have been the source of the audience's irritation. When the eighteenth-century playwright had attempted to refashion the less known theme of *La Princesse d'Elide*, for example, no such change in public reaction was recorded.

To be sure, *Les Sincères* is, almost as much as *Les Fausses confidences*, generally considered by critics to be an example of the author's last outburst of genius and certainly the product of an experienced, mature playwright's pen. It is, in fact, perhaps with the exception of *L'Epreuve*, the last play of consequence in Marivaux's theater. Yet, as the following comparisons will show, even at such a late stage in his career the dramatist did not find it impractical to remember the great heritage of his predecessor. The plot of the comedy, it will be recalled, deals with the inflexibly frank conduct of Ergaste and of the Marquise, the couple being drawn together by their apparent dislike of the artificial in human behavior. Soon their marriage is in sight. Frontin, however, the valet of Ergaste, pulls the latter into a trap by asking him to pass judgment on the comparative beauty of Araminte, former fiancée of his master, and the Marquise. When Ergaste votes in favor of Araminte, the Marquise loses her taste for sincerity and declares her determination to marry Dorante, her former fiancé, and Ergaste will marry the almost-jilted Araminte.

The general, basic similarity lies, of course, in the fact that both *Le Misanthrope* and *Les Sincères* deal with the dangers as well as the impossibility of telling the truth in every circumstance. And more often than not, critical comments on *Les Sincères* have been limited to underscoring this general similarity. Ferdinand Brunetière, for example, mentioned parenthetically that Marivaux had wanted, in general, to "refaire telle et telle pièce de Molière, et non pas *Le Sicilien* ou *Le Mariage forcé*, mais tout bonnement . . . *Le Misanthrope* dans *Les Sincères*."[1] It might be assumed that Brunetière considered Marivaux daring in the selection of his sources, but lack of elaboration in the criticism does not allow a definite conclusion. Suffice it to say that he has noticed a general resemblance between the two plays, but that he has not fully compared the plots (the article in which the statement appeared is, after all, concerned more with Marivaux's theater as a whole than with *Les Sincères* in particular) and the dialogues in order to prove by textual examples the validity of whatever he wished to imply in the verb *refaire*. Marcel Arland precedes a discussion of the innovations brought by the playwright to the plot of *Le Misanthrope* with an astonishing comment that betrays, perhaps, a lack of appreciation of the author's endeavor in *Les Sincères*: "Plus fâcheux pour la pièce, le souvenir du *Misanthrope*."[2] But then he continues: "Nous voilà au coeur de la pièce, et nous découvrons à la fois comment l'auteur s'inspire de Molière et comment il suit son propos personnel. L'invention de Marivaux est d'avoir fait de Célimène la réplique d'Alceste, si bien qu'il ne s'agit plus d'un conflit entre la franchise et l'artifice, mais du heurt de sincérités égales, et, finalement, de leur impossible exercice."[3] Thus, according to Arland, Molière's topic is Alceste versus the world; whereas Marivaux's subject is Ergaste versus the Marquise, that is, sincerity versus sincerity, an incompatibility of two forces, which does not enter at all in *Le Misanthrope*. Jean Fleury, for his part, agreed with Brunetière when he wrote, "L'idée de celle-ci [*Les Sincères*] a dû lui être suggérée par l'ambition de refaire le *Misanthrope*."[4] Gustave Larroumet also saw the connection between *Les Sincères* and Molière's play, but did so merely in a footnote and without any elaboration.[5] On the contrary, Arthur Tilley was much more specific. He noticed not only that *Les Sincères* is an unusual comedy on the part of Marivaux inasmuch as it deals with the psychology of falling out of love rather than that of falling in, but, "it is also interesting on account of its debt to Molière. For it not only owes its governing idea to *Le Misanthrope* but it reproduces the famous scene of the portraits. Unfortunately the Marquise is not a Célimène, and her portraits are prosaic and laboured compared with Célimène's brilliant improvisations. Ergaste too is a very inferior Alceste."[6] Kenneth N.

[1] Brunetière, "Marivaux et Molière," 675.
[2] Arland, *Marivaux*, 136.
[3] *Ibid.*, 138.
[4] Fleury, *Marivaux et le marivaudage*, 117.
[5] Larroumet, *Marivaux, sa vie et ses oeuvres*, 175.
[6] Tilley, *Three French Dramatists*, 111.

McKee belittled the importance of *Le Misanthrope* as a source by devoting less than one full sentence to it,[7] and E. J. H. Greene complained: "There have been many critics, in the last century or so, who have imagined that *Les Sincères* is Marivaux's challenge to *Le Misanthrope*." And then he argued that "the comparison with Molière is a red herring, one that should be thrown out."[8] On the other hand, the late Robert Kemp, noted critic of *Le Monde*, on the occasion of a recent *reprise* of Marivaux's play, made it known that he considered Marivaux's play "comme une suite du *Misanthrope*, la Marquise n'étant qu'une Célimène un peu plus âgée et Ergaste une copie d'Alceste."[9] This is, perhaps, an exaggerated statement, for as will be shown, there are enough differences between the plots and characters of the two comedies to refute any implication of direct plagiarism on the part of the eighteenth-century dramatist. But if the detractors have gone too far, the *aficionados* have not gone far enough, because there is much in *Les Sincères* that can be traced to *Le Misanthrope*.

The very beginning of Marivaux's play reminds one of parts of the first scene in Molière's. Alceste, who had described himself as follows:

Je veux qu'on soit sincère, et qu'en homme d'honneur
On ne lâche aucun mot qui ne parte du coeur . . .
Je veux qu'on me distingue (I, 1)

must have been present in Marivaux's memory, for he has Frontin describe his master in comparable terms: "Il dit ce qu'il pense de tout le monde . . . et ce n'est pas par malice qu'il est sincère, c'est qu'il a mis son affection à se distinguer par là . . . son but n'est pas de persuader qu'il vaut mieux que les autres, mais qu'il est autrement fait qu'eux, qu'il ne ressemble qu'à lui" (Scene 1). It is noteworthy that both playwrights use the verb *se distinguer*, and that Frontin's elaboration, which follows it, summarizes the analysis of Alceste by a number of recent commentators of Molière's play.[10]

The question of a law suit is also common to the beginning of both comedies.

PHILINTE: Ma foi, vous ferez bien de garder le silence.
          Contre votre partie éclatez un peu moins,
          Et donnez au procès une part de vos soins.

ALCESTE: Je n'en donnerai point, c'est une chose dite.

PHILINTE: Mais qui voulez-vous donc qui pour vous solicite?

[7]McKee, *Theater of Marivaux*, 225.
[8]Greene, *Marivaux*, 221-222.
[9]Robert Kemp, "*Les Sincères*," *Le Monde* (Paris), 16 September 1950, p. 23.
[10]For example: Lionel Gossman, *Men and Masks: A Study of Molière* (Baltimore: The Johns Hopkins Press, 1963), 85; J. D. Hubert, *Molière and the Comedy of Intellect* (Los Angeles: University of California Press, 1963), 141-145.

ALCESTE: Qui je veux? La raison, mon bon droit, l'équité.

PHILINTE: Aucun juge par vous ne sera visité?

ALCESTE: Non. Est-ce que ma cause est injuste ou douteuse?

PHILINTE: J'en demeure d'accord: mais la brigue est fâcheuse. Et . . .

ALCESTE: Non. J'ai résolu de n'en pas faire un pas. J'ai tort ou j'ai raison.

PHILINTE: Ne vous y fiez pas.

ALCESTE: Je ne remuerai point.

PHILINTE: Votre partie est forte. Et peut, par sa cabale, entraîner . . .

ALCESTE: Il n'importe.

PHILINTE: Vous vous tromperez.

ALCESTE: Soit . . . J'aurai le plaisir de perdre mon procès.

PHILINTE: Mais enfin . . .

ALCESTE: Je verrai dans cette plaiderie
Si les hommes auront assez d'effronterie,
Seront assez méchants, scélérats, et pervers,
Pour me faire injustice aux yeux de l'univers.

PHILINTE: Quel homme!

ALCESTE: Je voudrais, m'en coûtât-il grand'chose,
Pour la beauté du fait, avoir perdu ma cause. (I, 1)

In Marivaux's play, Ergaste is likewise engaged in a lawsuit that he strives to lose, and, in effect, he does. Frontin informs us that, "L'autre jour, un homme contre qui il avait un procès presque sûr vint lui dire: 'Tenez, ne plaidons plus; jugez vous-même, je vous prends pour arbitre, je m'y engage.' Là-dessus, voilà mon homme qui s'allume de la vanité d'être extraordinaire; le voilà qui pèse, qui prononce gravement contre lui, et qui perd son procès pour gagner la réputation de s'être condamné lui-même: il fut huit jours enivré du bruit que cela fit dans le monde" (Scene 1). It is notable that 1) both *sincères* have a law suit on their hands; 2) their cause is just; and 3) both make somewhat similar efforts in attempting to lose. Alceste refuses to *garder le silence* and Philinte accuses him of speaking against his own case (line two of his speech above), while Ergaste *s'allume de la vanité d'être extraordinaire* and *prononce gravement contre lui*. Moreover, both Alceste and Ergaste see in losing a strong affirmation of their greatness, a worthy compensation for whatever sums of money or other material goods may have been involved.

Three scenes later, Marivaux recalls an even more important episode of *Le Misanthrope*, the celebrated portrait scene of the second act. The brilliant discussion of Molière's counterfeiters (Célimène, Clitandre, Acaste, Philinte) is not reproduced as such in the one-act eighteenth-century piece. Instead, Marivaux summarizes and/or borrows some of the characteristics of the people criticized by Molière's personages. For example, the following piece of dialogue in *Le Misanthrope:*

> ACASTE: Parbleu! s'il faut parler des gens extravagants,
>   Je viens d'en essuyer un des plus fatigants;
>   Damon le raisonneur, qui m'a ne vous déplaise,
>   Une heure au grand soleil, tenu hors de ma chaise.
>
> CELIMENE: C'est un parleur étrange, et qui trouve toujours
>   L'art de ne vous rien dire avec de grands discours (II, 5)

is duplicated in the Marquise's description of an aquaintance's magniloquence: "Notre cercle finissait par un petit homme . . . qui ne dit rien et qui parle toujours; c'est-à-dire qu'il a . . . la parole éternelle" (Scene 4). Moreover, Célimène's sketch of Adraste

> Ah! quel orgueil extrême!
> C'est un homme gonflé de l'amour de soi-même.
> Son mérite jamais n'est content. (II, 5)

likewise is matched by the Marquise's delineation of a similarly self-enamored person: "L'un était un jeune homme . . . un fat toujours agité du plaisir de se sentir fait comme il est. . . . Imaginez-vous qu'il n'a précisément qu'un objet dans la pensée, c'est de se montrer" (Scene 4).

Other lines of *Les Sincères* must have been suggested to Marivaux by certain episodes in *Le Misanthrope*. For example, Alceste, who witnesses the portraits mentioned, revolts against his friends' gossip. He complains:

> C'est que jamais, morbleu! les hommes n'ont raison . . .
> Et que je vois qu'ils sont, sur toutes les affaires,
> Loueurs impertinents, ou censeurs téméraires. (II, 5)

When Philinte reminds Alceste that the people the group is criticizing do not enjoy Alceste's admiration either, the latter agrees, "Plus on aime quelqu'un, moins il faut qu'on le flatte; / A ne rien pardonner le pur amour éclate." And Célimène concludes:

> Enfin, s'il faut qu'à vous s'en rapportent les coeurs,
> On doit, pour bien aimer, renoncer aux douceurs,
> Et du parfait amour mettre l'honneur suprême
> A bien injurier les personnes qu'on aime. (II, 5)

Thus, just as Alceste's sincerity had caused Célimène to reach this conclusion, so too, Ergaste's frankness[11] causes the Marquise to think that she has been insulted by him. "Eh! savais-je, moi, que j'étais vaine, laide et mutine? Vous me l'apprenez" (Scene 14). It is noteworthy that Marivaux not only inserts in his play a portrait scene, but also

---

[11]See Scene 12, in which Ergaste admits that Araminte is more beautiful than the Marquise.

that some of the portraits are alike, and that the Marquise (although unlike Célimène because the latter does not claim to practice inflexible sincerity in her acts) arrives at the same conclusion about Ergaste as Célimène did about Alceste, that is, that both men hold it as an *honneur suprême / A bien injurier les personnes qu'on aime*.

But more than the individual portraits, it is the entire tone of Marivaux's scene that makes it a simple reorchestration of the familiar *moliéresque* theme. Marcel Arland admitted that "il [the souvenir of *Le Misanthrope*] nous suit jusque dans la galerie des portraits,"[12] and even E. J. H. Greene, in spite of his statement quoted earlier, agreed that "the comedy of comparisons has gone beyond the stage, generally to Marivaux's disadvantage: his portrait scene has been taken to be an imitation of Molière's."[13] The fact is that only one critic, Gustave Attinger, has attempted to defend the eighteenth-century playwright. According to him, Marivaux's portraits are drawn more skillfully because there are in the Marquise's descriptions "beaucoup plus de liberté et de verve" and "les rosseries de la Marquise y sont coupées par des mots prêtés aux victimes elles-mêmes, et favorables aux jeux de scène."[14] The question is mainly one of personal preference, however. Although Attinger's statement is true as far as it goes, Molière's portraits have a more universal interest precisely because Célimène does not quote the persons whom she criticizes and thereby allows readers and spectators to associate more freely the descriptions with men and women of their own acquaintance. Another element that is conspicuously lacking from Marivaux's scene is the added attraction of Alceste's rising anger and indignation as he hears the idle prattle of Célimène. There is no clear-cut misanthropist in *Les Sincères,* and the youthful Ergaste does not intrigue nor amuse nearly so much as Molière's character.

There is finally one other similarity to be mentioned, that is, the one between III, 4 of *Le Misanthrope* and Scene 17 of *Les Sincères*. Arsinoé, who is annoyed at the fact that Alceste pays little attention to her, visits her friend, Célimène, and a conversation ensues in which the two women tell each other unpleasant *niceties* in a highly sarcastic, though polite manner. When at the end of the verbal battle Alceste appears, Célimène takes her leave by saying, "Il faut que j'aille écrire un mot de lettre / Que, sans me faire tort, je ne saurais remettre" (III, 4). The subtle quarrel that prompted Célimène's abrupt exit was caused by Arsinoé's relation of derogatory remarks she supposedly had heard

---

[12]Arland, *Marivaux*, 136.

[13]Greene, *Marivaux*, 221.

[14]Gustave Attinger, *L'Esprit de la commedia dell'arte dans le théâtre français* (Paris: Librairie Théâtrale, 1950), 394.

people make about her hostess. The fact that she claims not to have agreed with these remarks does not convince Célimène, who puts a stern end to the meeting. Marivaux's scene begins in the same manner: Araminte, the rival of the Marquise, informs the latter of a conversation in which her *friend's* character had been belittled. Like Arsinoé, she is quick to add that all along she had been on her side and had attempted to defend her. But the effect of such artificial reassurances is equal to that in Molière's play and, as in *Le Misanthrope*, Marivaux has the Marquise use the same excuse in order to precipitate an end to Araminte's visit: "De grâce, permettez-moi d'écrire un petit billet qui presse" (Scene 17).

It is clear, then, that a number of key scenes in *Le Misanthrope* have their counterpart in *Les Sincères*. Not only is there a basic similarity of plot, but often the specific situations, at times even the vocabulary, are essentially analogous. Thus, if one ignores the partial exaggeration for which Ferdinand Brunetière and Robert Kemp might be considered responsible, textual examples from the two plays seem to bear out the close resemblances noted by most critics and to contradict E. J. H. Greene's contention that the rapports between *Le Misanthrope* and *Les Sincères* constitute *a red herring*.

But if the *moliéresque* recollections are numerous, and if they do indeed occur in important scenes, there are also differences worth noting. The fact that Molière's topic is Alceste versus the world, and Marivaux's is Ergaste versus the Marquise has been pointed to already. In addition, it should be recalled that Alceste is totally inflexible and does not recognize any exaggeration in his behavior; he will not admit that he might be wrong; he is and remains a misanthropist. On the contrary, Ergaste agrees he could be wrong (Scene 18, for example); he is willing to compromise (Scene 20); and he does, in the end, allow his social awareness to dominate and vanquish whatever vague desire for isolation he may have had in the past, because he does decide to abandon his magnanimous scorn for women and marry the not always truthful but basically honest Araminte (Scene 21). Robert Kemp's supposition that the Marquise is a Célimène who has grown a few years older is not quite borne out by the events in the play. Actually, Célimène refuses to follow Alceste and persists in attempting to continue to lead an artificial existence; whereas the Marquise is persuaded to give up her artificial existence and to marry Dorante. Moreover, Marivaux's introduction of the Marquise as a female counterpart of Alceste, the evolution occurring in the character of Ergaste, and the Marquise's own return to a more reasonable social existence indicate that there is, nevertheless, a measure of originality in his comedy.

Only two other possible sources have been mentioned for *Les Sincères:* a little piece by Riccoboni entitled *Les Sincères à contretemps,* and a sketch in Marivaux's *L'Indigent philosophe.* The first is only a poor imitation of Molière's *Le Misanthrope,* and outside of the basic idea of a person bent on telling the truth at all times, it bears no specific similarities with Marivaux's play; the second is a portrait that the dramatist might have had in mind when he depicted Ergaste, but then the original description in *L'Indigent philosophe* is also an echo of the celebrated figure of Molière's hero, Alceste.

It is noteworthy that *Les Sincères* has had very few revivals. When it was presented on stage in recent times, in 1891, 1931, and 1950, it enjoyed only marginal receptions. The facts are that Marivaux's comedy is overshadowed by that of Molière; it lacks sparkle and is extremely slow-moving. Although the writer probably deserves credit for composing a play that deals with something besides the problem of nascent love (a *rara avis* in his case), the dialogue does not contain those usually catchy, typically Marivaldian lines that set it apart, in spite of the degree of imitation, from the *moliéresque* source. The conversations are often lifeless, at least cerebral to the point that they remain unconvincing and simply border on stylistic exercises. There is no warmth, no expression or manifestation of biological urges, and the play can probably be appreciated best in a reading effort than as a dramatic presentation. If Brunetière, by his criticism, meant only that Marivaux might have done better to imitate less known plays such as *Le Sicilien* or *Le Mariage forcé,* then he probably was correct, but in no way can *Les Sincères* be a challenge to *Le Misanthrope.* There is no engaging, enormously complex Célimène in Marivuax's play, and there is no deceived Alceste. Marivaux's personages learn from their errors and opt ultimately for tact, that is, for a middle way between hypocrisy and sincerity. So things turn out well, in the traditional Hollywood manner. The Marquise's final remark, "Ah! ah! ah! nous avons pris un plaisant détour pour arriver là" (Scene 21), summarizes the play and states properly its limitations. Outside of the fact that Marivaux apparently wished to restate the theme of *Le Misanthrope,* there appears to be no reason for the detour mentioned by the Marquise, nor for its length. Moreover, detours are almost always irritating, time-consuming, and do not advance the traveler, or the spectator, much beyond the initial starting point. Marivaux's characters reach a compromise and arrive at a happy solution: there is very little that is cathartic in such a turn of events. On the contrary, Molière's hero intrigues, disturbs, and makes one uneasy until the end of the play and even after. To use twentieth-century terminology, he does not become a "rhino" by joining the

crowds of tactful hypocrites, and his refusal of happiness at any cost
points to his superiority; there is much that is cathartic in the possibility of such considered and deliberate haughtiness.

L'EPREUVE

Once again, it was a Molière specialist, Emile Fabre and this time only one, who noted certain unspecified similarities between *L'Epreuve* and *La Princesse d'Elide*. In commenting on Molière's play, he declared that the eighteenth-century dramatist, in *L'Epreuve* ". . . mit aussi en présence des amoureux et dans chaque couple, tantôt la femme, tantôt l'homme, qui se donnent le singulier plaisir d'alarmer et de faire pleurer l'amante pour s'assurer de son obéissance et du don total de sa personne."[1] Although often presented (*L'Epreuve* being Marivaux's second most popular play after *Le Jeu de l'amour et du hasard*), neither those reviewers who were contemporaries of Marivaux, nor any commentator since mentioned *La Princesse d'Elide* as a possible source. As will be shown below, the recollections are not so numerous as in other instances in which Marivaux made use of them; yet, since *L'Epreuve* has been hailed as "one of the most beloved in his whole theater, one into which he poured the essence of his genius. . . . [A] poetic evocation of young lovers' feelings [in] its tender probing of their fears and desires . . . a work of superb artistry,"[2] it is significant that practically at every qualitative stage of his career Marivaux used, in various degrees, one facet or another of certain *moliéresque* themes.

There is little that is novel in *L'Epreuve*. The story concerns Angélique, who loves Lucidor, a rich young man with an inferiority complex, which prompts him to disbelieve that he might be loved for himself and instead makes him fear that the young girl's attentions are caused by the general knowledge of his wealth. Females are usually predatory, he seems to think, and one needs to make sure that financial reasons do not motivate their words of love. And so he hesitates and refuses, temporarily, to respond to Angélique's friendly words and gestures. Not without a bit of cruelty,[3] he proposes another husband for her, Frontin, his valet, whom he disguises as a debonair Parisian. But no sooner is this scheme arranged than a peasant appears, Blaise, who would like to marry Angélique for the small dowry she has at her disposal. In an additional effort to test Angélique's love, Lucidor supports Blaise. Following the girl's rejection of the pretender, Frontin is introduced and, to the despair of Madame Argante, the mother, Angélique dismisses politely the newly projected husband. The young

---

[1] Fabre, *Molière*, 194.

[2] McKee, *Theater of Marivaux*, 231.

[3] This aspect of Lucidor has been belabored by numerous critics: Jules Lemaître, for example, in *Les Annales politiques et littéraires* (Paris, 1890), 15, 120; Gabriel Marcel in *Les Nouvelles littéraires, artistiques et scientifiques*, 3(21 February 1946): 5; and others.

girl's persistent refusal to marry anyone else, under the eyes of the increasingly pleased Lucidor who contemplates the reaction of the girl each time that a *parti* is introduced, makes him finally declare his love, and provide the happy ending of the play.

To be sure, Marivuax's plot is different from that of *La Princesse d'Elide*. Nevertheless, there are in *L'Epreuve* two situations that show a resemblance to Molière's play. The first bears on the scene in which the Princess, who would like to subdue the heart of Euryale, tests him by suggesting that she is about to marry: "Prince . . . le mérite d'un prince m'a frappé aujourd'hui les yeux; et mon âme tout d'un coup, comme par un miracle, est devenue sensible aux traits de cette passion que j'avais toujours méprisée" (IV, 1). Hoping that she will make it clear that the prince she wants to marry is Euryale, she continues: "Mais encore, pour qui souhaiteriez-vous que je me dé- clarasse? . . . Hé bien! prince, je veux bien vous la [her choice] découvrir. Je suis sûre que vous allez approuver mon choix" (IV, 1). Yielding, however, to her spite, she names the prince of Messène. Similarly, Lucidor presents to Angélique a young man, Frontin, whom he claims to have brought from Paris for the purpose of marrying him to her: "En allant chez votre mère, j'ai trouvé Monsieur qui arrivait, et j'ai cru qu'il n'y avait rien de plus pressé que de vous l'amener: c'est lui, c'est ce mari pour qui vous vous êtes si favorablement prévenue, et qui . . ." (Scene 10). Despite himself (because if Angélique realizes it is Lucidor who wants to marry her, not Frontin, then the test fails to prove anything), he continues: "Par le rapport de nos caractères, il [Frontin] est en effet un autre moi-même" (Scene 10). Of course, this line corresponds to the Princess' *Je suis sûre que vous allez approuver mon choix*. Won, later on, not by spite as in the case of the Princess, but by the awareness that the test would not be efficacious otherwise, Lucidor goes on to say: "Il m'a apporté aussi le portrait d'une jeune et jolie personne qu'on veut me faire épouser à Paris. . . . Jetez les yeux dessus: comment la trouvez-vous?" (Scene 10). And then he insists on Angélique's marriage to his friend: "Vous savez, belle Angélique, que je vous ai d'abord consultée sur ce mariage; je n'y ai pensé que par zèle pour vous, et vous m'en avez paru satisfaite" (Scene 16). Here Lucidor refers to a previous conversation with Angèlique in which he had, in effect, consulted her on the projected marriage (Scene 8), knowing, of course, that the marriage Angélique had in mind was with Lucidor. This is hardly different from the scene just quoted from *La Princesse d'Elide* in which the Princess had consulted Euryale on the advisability of her own marriage with someone else. Once again, therefore, Lucidor seems to be doing exactly what Emile Fabre had noted, that is, taking pleasure in alarming the girl he loves in order to be sure of her total amorous devotion. Moreover, Lucidor's action can be compared not only with that of the Princess consulting Euryale, but also with that of Euryale consulting the Princess on his own projected marriage with Aglante.

The second resemblance emerges from a comparison between the episode in which Iphitas, the Princess' father, declares that it is time his daughter confess her love for Euryale, and Scene 18 of Marivaux's play. In Molière's comedy, the spiteful Princess exclaims: "Je l'aime, dites-vous? et vous m'imputez cette lâcheté! O ciel! quelle est mon infortune! Puis-je bien sans mourir, entendre ces paroles? Et faut-il que je sois si malheureuse, qu'on me soupçonne de l'aimer?" (V, 2). Likewise, in Marivaux's play, when Maître Blaise, one of the husbands proposed by Lucidor and rejected by Angélique, suggests to the latter that she is in love with Lucidor, the young girl becomes indignant: "Comment? Ne le croyez pas; vous ne seriez pas un homme de bien de le croire. M'accuser d'aimer. . . . Vous m'accablez. . . . J'ai donc le coeur bien bas, bien misérable! Ah! que l'affront qu'on me fait m'est sensible!" (Scene 18). Angélique's statements reflect those of the Princess: they reveal the same juvenile wrath, the same spite.

Only one Marivaux specialist has mentioned another source for *L'Epreuve*, Kenneth N. McKee, who indicated Destouches' *Le Curieux impertinent*. He did so in a footnote only, and without any specificity.[4] A close reading of the two plays reveals, indeed, that Lucidor's attempts to test Angélique may be traced to the similar efforts of Léandre in *Le Curieux impertinent*, the only difference being that Lucidor has a valet, Frontin, court Angélique, whereas Léandre entrusts his friend, Damon, with the courting of his girl. Frontin's words of caution to Léandre in the sense that he might end up by causing Angélique to fall in love with him (Scene 1) also are expressed by Damon, who displays an even greater reticence in going ahead with the projected test (I, 7); Lucidor's *feinte* of being about to marry another girl in Paris (Scene 10) already had been used as a test by Léandre (V, 2); nevertheless, the semitragic ending of *Le Curieux impertinent* has not influenced Marivaux, nor is the elaborate servant subplot to be found in *L'Epreuve*. It is quite possible, however, that Destouches' source, in the scenes mentioned, was also *La Princesse d'Elide*, for he did not find it impractical, on occasion, to follow *moliéresque* examples.

All this is not to say, however, that Marivaux relied on *La Princesse d'Elide* as much as in the past, and one may almost agree with Kenneth N. McKee, who sees the originality of *L'Epreuve* in

[4]McKee, *Theater of Marivaux*, 232.

"Angélique . . . one of Marivaux's most enchanting heroines. Tender in her love, poignant in her suffering, she is not angry at Lucidor for having subjected her to the tests. She is glad to give these proofs of her love, and seeks no retaliation. . . . [and in] the poetic beauty of the love scenes, the subtle probings of the heart, the bouncing gaiety of the servants, all blending"[5] in a masterful work. As in the case of Araminte of *Les Fausses confidences,* the inventiveness of Marivaux, whatever there is of it, should be traced to his depiction of the heroine and to some of her typically Marivaldian speeches. Like her predecessor, Angélique is one of those women born with unusual tact and kindness. She is unable to get angry either at the words and deeds of a domineering mother, or at the sometimes infantile, sometimes cruel tests to which she is submitted by the man she loves. On the contrary, the shortcomings of those in her entourage spur her on to additional displays of understanding and good-natured responses. Consider, for example, the *quid pro quo* in which Lucidor describes to the young girl the husband he has picked out for her, leading her to believe that he is speaking of himself.

> ANGELIQUE: . . . Ah ça, ne me trompez pas, au moins, tout le coeur me bat; loge-t-il avec vous?
>
> LUCIDOR: Oui, Angélique, nous sommes dans la même maison.
>
> ANGELIQUE: Ce n'est pas assez, je n'ose encore être bien aise en toute confiance. Quel homme est-ce?
>
> LUCIDOR: Un homme très riche.
>
> ANGELIQUE: Ce n'est pas là le principal. Après?
>
> LUCIDOR: Il est de mon âge et de ma taille.
>
> ANGELIQUE: Bon: c'est ce que je voulais savoir.
>
> LUCIDOR: Nos caractères se ressemblent: il pense comme moi.
>
> ANGELIQUE: Toujours de mieux en mieux. Que je l'aimerai!
>
> LUCIDOR: C'est un homme tout aussi uni, tout aussi sans façon que je le suis.
>
> ANGELIQUE: Je n'en veux point d'autre.
>
> LUCIDOR: Qui n'a ni ambition, ni gloire, et qui n'exigera de celle qu'il épousera que son coeur.
>
> ANGELIQUE, *riant:* Il l'aura, Monsieur Lucidor, il l'aura; il l'a déjà; je l'aime autant que vous, ni plus ni moins. (Scene 8)

Of such an innocent ingenuity Molière's Princess could not have been ever capable. Consider, also, her reaction of delicate firmness to the advances of one of the pretenders, Frontin (a reaction of which Marivaux's pen is so often capable).

[5]*Ibid.,* 235-236.

Je vous dirai donc, Monsieur, que je serais mortifiée s'il fallait vous aimer; le coeur me le dit; on sent cela. Non que vous ne soyez fort aimable, pourvu que ce ne soit pas moi qui vous aime; je ne finirai point de vous louer quand ce sera pour une autre; je vous prie de prendre en bonne part ce que je vous dis là; j'y vais de tout mon coeur; ce n'est pas moi qui ai été vous chercher, une fois; je ne songeais pas à vous, et si je l'avais pu, il ne m'en aurait pas plus coûté de vous crier: 'Ne venez pas!' que de vous dire: 'Allez-vous-en.' (Scene 16)

But perhaps nowhere more than in the scene in which Lucidor finally declares his love is the heroine more enchanting, while at the same time holding on, shakily, to just the proper amount of expected feminine shyness by not using the word *love*, rather confirming her long-stifled passion with a simple question.

LUCIDOR: Et si je restais, si je vous demandais votre main, si nous ne nous quittions de la vie?

ANGELIQUE: Voilà du moins ce qu'on appelle parler, cela.

LUCIDOR: Vous m'aimez donc?

ANGELIQUE: Ai-je jamais fait autre chose? (Scene 21)

Unlike the infinitely more spiteful and rancor-filled Princess, Angélique is only too glad to give no thought to recriminations and to respond in tender and telling terms. This is the originality of the eighteenth-century playwright, albeit obscured here and there by repetitive *moliéresque* recollections.

FELICIE

Marivaux's last play to be considered here was not presented on the stage until 1960, when the director of *L'Equipe* came up with the idea of turning it into a ballet. The success was moderate, but *Félicie* has not been shown since. The play was read in 1757 by a group of French comedians, and apparently was liked enough to be accepted by the Comédie. However, the author must have had second thoughts caused either by his own misgivings concerning the quality of the play, or by the suspected lack of sincerity in the acceptance by the Comédie, for he withdrew his work. Whatever the case, no reviewer has had much good to say about *Félicie,* and only one has mentioned a *moliéresque* source for it.

Félicie is an allegorical morality, the theme of which is simplicity itself. The heroine has been raised by a fairy who is able to give to her one gift. She chooses beauty, and she gets it. Because beauty may be dangerous, Modestie becomes Félicie's companion. In the course of a party, Lucidor flirts with Félicie while being introduced, and in spite of Modestie, who attempts to intervene, the heroine is just about ready to consent to the young man's pressing demands. Diane, who, strangely enough, in this play represents virtue, comes to the help of Modestie, and the two goddesses help Félicie resist the man's advances. Coquetry, then, when *benefiting* from beauty, can only lead a girl to submission, Marivaux appears to imply, were it not for the aid of wiser, if insipid interventions.

Félicie's plot has little to do, then, with any of Molière's plays. Nevertheless, even at the end of his theatrical career, Marivaux apparently did not find it possible, or practical, to steer totally clear of *moliéresque* reminiscences. In this case, it is Molière's first major success, *Les Précieuses ridicules,* that Marivaux had in mind for one or two episodes in his play. The first is probably the result of an involuntary recollection, but since it has been noted (without significant comment) by one of Marivaux's critics,[1] it should be mentioned in this context. It occurs in one of Félicie's speeches to Modestie: "Il faut que l'obscurité soit mon partage! Que ne m'a-t-on dit que c'était le plus grand malheur du monde d'être jolie, puisqu'il faut être esclave des conséquences de son visage?" (Scene 3). About this passage Pierre Duviquet remarked: "*Etre esclave des conséquences de son visage,* c'est une phrase qui rappelle malheureusement celles de Cathos et de Magdelon dans *Les Précieuses ridicules.*[2] Nevertheless, a thorough

---

[1] See following discussion.
[2] Duviquet ed., *Oeuvres complètes,* 2, 448.

reading of Molière's play does not reveal a similar line in the speeches of Cathos or of Magdelon. What the critic evidently meant to say was that this type of *précieux* discourse is reminiscent of the general tone of Cathos and Magdelon.

The second instance of similarity occurs between Scene 10 of Molière's play, and Scene 7 of *Félicie*. It will be recalled that in *Les Précieuses ridicules* Mascarille attempts to amuse Cathos and Magdelon by an impromptu he composes:

Oh! oh! je n'y prenais pas garde:
Tandis que, sans songer à mal, je vous regarde,
Votre oeil en tapinois me dérobe mon coeur.
Au voleur! au voleur! au voleur! (Scene 10)

And in Scene 14 he proceeds to sing to the sound of violins. Likewise in *Félicie*, in his attempts to woo the heroine, Lucidor has the hunters who serve him sing and dance for the young girl they have just met. To facilitate a quicker acceptance by Félicie, the hero then takes part himself in the show that he has organized. He declares, "Ils n'auront pas seuls l'honneur de vous amuser, et je prétends y avoir part" (Scene 7). And he sings:

De vos beaux yeux le charme inévitable
Me fait brûler de la plus vive ardeur:
Plus que Diane redoutable,
Sans flèche ni carquois, vous tirez droit au coeur.
(Scene 7)

Lucidor, like Mascarille, composes verses for the girl he courts. It is notable that the stanza of each suffers from faulty metrics. Mascarille complained of his heart being stolen; Lucidor bemoans the fact that he had his shot at. It is also notable that Mascarille's heart was stolen by the eye of the girl *en tapinois*, whereas that of Lucidor was shot at by the eyes of Félicie *sans flèche ni carquois*, that is to say *en tapinois* also.

It is true, of course, that some of the episodes cited may be considered part of the common dramatic fund of the period. The objection may be raised, therefore, that they were not borrowed necessarily from Molière. Nevertheless, Pierre Duviquet remarked: "*Sans flèche ni carquois, vous tirez droit au coeur. C'est encore là du Mascarille ou du Jodelet tout pur.*"[3] What matters is less whether Marivaux's tone in *Félicie* is at times deliberately *moliéresque*, than the fact that, even at the end of his career, he is believed by some to have sought and received inspiration from the seventeenth-century master. Even when the rapports between Marivaux and Molière are few and comparatively unimportant, they add to the total picture, which is one of continued

[3]*Ibid.*, 2, 461.

remembrance of vocabulary, manner of expression, and situations found in the comedies of his predecessor.

What matters, also, is the fact that, when Marivaux attempts to preach, as he does in *Félicie, moliéresque* tone and episodes fail to make the play palatable. Whereas Molière was content simply to point to how easy it is to impress young, provincial girls who play at being coquettish with song, dance, and verses without thereby eliciting the sympathy of spectators or readers, Marivaux commits the error of catering to the prudish by suggesting that the blend of beauty and feminine coquetry can ruin not only a girl's reputation but the girl herself. One has to be suspicious, he seems to say, to counsel constantly, indeed to save such girls. Marivaux's concern for morality damages the play. On the contrary, Molière's more limited, yet more strategically theatrical aim is to cause one to laugh at young females whose combination of looks and flirtatious attitudes make them immensely gullible. Molière is not concerned with saving such girls, witness the unlikeable character of the father, Gorgibus, who attempts to convert Magdelon and Cathos to reasonableness, most of the time unsuccessfully. He is no match for Modestie nor for Diane, the superhuman forces who snatch Félicie away from the forthcoming fall and give to the play a Hollywood ending.

Moliéresque recollections or not, *Félicie* was reviewed so poorly that even admirers of Marivaux found it difficult to say anything complimentary about it. Jean Fleury, for example, wrote: "L'auteur a voulu montrer sans doute que sans La Modestie le don de plaire est dangereux parce qu'il expose à la tentation. . . . La piéce, du reste, est faible de tout point. Les développements manquent, et le style tourne à la sécheresse."[4] Gustave Larroumet labeled it facetiously a *moralité*,[5] and Marcel Arland himself, usually so friendly to the eighteenth-century playwright, called *Félicie* "une bluette de patronage mondain."[6] Only E. J. H. Greene attempted valiantly to compliment Marivaux's effort.

> For over two centuries, this play has been dismissed as insipid and therefore negligible. The decency of Marivaux's language and the allegorical form tend to disguise the fact that it deals with a crucial moment in the life of a sensitive adolescent girl. Félicie is much like the Angéliques of *L'Ecole des Mères* and *La Mère confidente*, but instead of a Mme Argante (whether harsh or tender), she has a trio of abstract semi-deities organizing her conduct in advance, no less surely. By definition, a deity always wins against humans in the long run, and the case of

[4]Fleury, *Marivaux et le marivaudage*, 245.
[5]Larroumet, *Marivaux, sa vie et ses oeuvres*, 245.
[6]Arland, *Marivaux*, 148.

Félicie is no exception. This is another way of saying that the play lacks dramatic interest.[7]

But no matter, for his conclusion, too, corroborates the host of poor commentaries that *Félicie* received throughout the centuries.

The play, then, one of Marivaux's last efforts, is in no way aided by the author's persistent, if reduced, *moliéresque* inspiration.

[7]Greene, *Marivaux*, 265-266.

CONCLUSION

Marivaux, then, was influenced by Molière. This influence, in its various degrees, has been shown in sixteen of his plays, that is to say, in almost half of the total theatrical production of the eighteenth-century playwright.

It is notable that the individual plays are representative of the different periods of Marivaux's career: *Le Père prudent et équitable* is characteristic of the unpolished and inexperienced beginning of the writer; *Arlequin poli par l'amour, La Surprise de l'amour, Le Dénouement imprévu, La (Seconde) Surprise de l'amour, Les Serments indiscrets, L'Heureux stratagème, Les Fausses confidences,* and *L'Epreuve* represent the surprise-type play, and at the same time are characteristic of the middle and climactic periods of his professional life; *L'Héritier du village, L'Ile de la raison, Le Triomphe de Plutus, L'Ecole de mères, La Mère confidente,* and *Les Sincères* are samples of his social comedies and belong also to his middle and climactic periods; finally, *Félicie* represents the anticlimax of Marivaux's career.[1]

It probably would be pointless to evaluate Marivaux's efforts on the basis of degree of *moliéresque* influence. This influence was extensive in *La Surprise de l'amour* and in *Les Fausses confidences,* for example, yet (or perhaps because of it) these comedies generally are considered among the best in Marivaux's repertory. The number of *reprises* and critical approvals bears witness to their quality. On the other hand, Molière's influence was rather minor, by comparison, in *Le Triomphe de Plutus* and in *Félicie,* yet (or perhaps because of it) these comedies are inconsequential: the author refused to sign the first, and the second was performed on the stage only as a ballet. It is also true that other plays, such as *L'Hériter du village* and *Les Serments indiscrets,* in which the *moliéresque* influence appears prominently, generally are considered poor plays, both by audiences and critics. Conversely, *Arlequin poli par l'amour* and *L'Epreuve,* for example, in which the *moliéresque* source of inspiration is only minor, are considered successful theater in the eighteenth and twentieth centuries. From all this, it is difficult to reach conclusions, and unnecessary as well. What matters more than anything else is to begin to disregard d'Alembert's reports concerning Marivaux's alleged dislike for the theater of Molière, and to stop ignoring the presence of the seventeenth-century master, variable as it

---

[1] Needless to say, this classification of types of plays is arbitrary; one and the same play belongs at times to more than one classification and, as a matter of fact, Marivaux's critics differ in their grouping of his comedies.

is, in the comedies of Marivaux.

This presence, of course, points only to the fact that either D'Alembert's reports are erroneous, or simply that Marivaux did not wish to acknowledge his debt to Molière. If it detracts at all from the value of his comedies, it does so to a degree only: the playwright's inventiveness suffers. The individual plays in which the *moliéresque* recollections occur at times profit from, at others are diminished by the measure of remembrance. But if there is one thing that Marivaux did not manage to extract from Molière, it is his predecessor's ability to philosophize by means of irony, caricature, and ridicule. In this connection, Kenneth N. McKee observes:

> For example, Molière believed that fathers should not force incompatible marriages on their children, but instead of presenting liberal-minded fathers on the stage, he ridiculed obstinate ones such as M. Orgon in *Le Tartuffe*, Harpagon in *L'Avare*, and M. Jourdain in *Le Bourgeois gentilhomme*. Marivaux, on the other hand, presented his philosophy with disarming simplicity. If he had a point to make, he went straight to the heart of the matter and expressed his conviction as an integral part of the text without deviousness.[2]

But what is missing from such comments is recognition that one of the reasons Molière's comedies is superior resides precisely in the *deviousness* of his approach: it is one that is much more bound to make for laughter than *disarming simplicity*. One might add that preachers make a point, writers of comedies go around it, suggest it, but are never any more presumptuous than that.

All this is not to say that Marivaux knowingly preaches, or even that he does so frequently. The fact remains, nevertheless, that he is much less able than was his predecessor to cause heartfelt, loud laughter. When he does show such a capability, more often than not it is a peasant or a servant who makes one laugh. Most of his other characters are simply content to bring a smile to the spectator's lips, and even the origin of that is intellectual only. If Marivaux may be praised for having abandoned most of the post-Molière crude language and abuse of farcical situations as a means to comicality, it also must be acknowledged that his comedies are less apt to induce that purging, cathartic result that a buoyant, uninhibited mirth produces.

From the point of view of content, Marivaux's inventiveness resides in his depiction of the topography of the heart. In the more classical plays of Molière, love always played a diminished role: it was usually born before the initial curtain and, once acknowledged, it did not constitute the plot of the comedy, rather it served the loftier ends of the author, who laughed, ridiculed, or attacked various human shortcom-

[2]McKee, *Theater of Marivaux*, 259-260.

ings. Love rarely came to the forefront and hardly ever was traced, analyzed, or judged either by the lovers themselves or those around them (the comments on love by parents and/or tutors were not designed to explain the feeling, rather to obliterate it). On the contrary, love is a map, Marivaux appears to imply, and he becomes its geographer. He points to the source, to its growing pains as it struggles through mountainous detours and dangerous pits, to the roads it must cross, and the inroads attempted by timidity, parental opposition, financial or social considerations, and other such obstacles. But the stream eventually flows into the ocean, much as the shepherdess is able, ultimately, to join the shepherd in the *Carte du tendre*. What one misses in the way of sparkling jocularity and ensuing catharsis resulting from Molière's plays is made up, to an extent, by Marivaux's explanations of the casuistry of gallantry and coquetry. The analyst of sentiment and dissector of the heart that he was, Marivaux went beyond *moliéresque* limits, and broadened the playwright's scope into areas heretofore largely ignored by writers of comedies and only touched upon by composers of tragedies.

From the point of view of style, the originality of the eighteenth-century playwright consists, even in those plays that show a *moliéresque* inspiration, in his ability to use a form of expression suitable to the depiction of shades and nuances of feeling. The accusation of *marivaudage*, which was brought against such a style, as previously shown,[3] is only partly valid. Monotonous though the frequently long speeches of Marivaux's characters may be at times, detailed explanations and summaries add to the reader's comprehension. This makes up somewhat for the liveliness and brio of Molière's language, which Marivaux, for the most part, was incapable of or found impractical to emulate. This is also one of the reasons why some of the comedies of the eighteenth-century playwright provide for more pleasurable reading than for successful stage presentations.

One need not push the comparison any further. Next to the vigor of Molière one might be tempted to see only the pallor of Marivaux. Yet that probably would be the case in a comparison between most playwrights and the seventeenth-century master. Marivaux can and does stand on his own feet. But in spite of what he is reported to have said and thought of Molière, in many of his plays he relied upon episodes and themes made famous by his predecessor.

[3]See Preface and Introduction.

BIBLIOGRAPHY

Alembert, Jean le Rond d'. "Eloge de Marivaux," *Marivaux Théâtre*, edited by Bernard Dort. Paris: Le Club Français du Livre, 1961.

Argens, Jean-Baptiste, Marquis d'. *Réflexions historiques et critiques sur le goût*. Paris: Marquis d'Argens, 1743.

Arland, Marcel, *Marivaux*. Paris: Gallimard, 1950.

Attinger, Gustave. *L'Esprit de la commedia dell'arte dans le théâtre français*. Paris: Librairie Théâtrale, 1950.

Brady, Valentini Papadopoulou. *Love in the Theatre of Marivaux: A Study of the Factors Influencing Its Birth, Development and Expression*. Geneva: Droz, 1970.

Brunetière, Ferdinand. "Marivaux et Molière." *Revue des deux mondes* (1 April 1881):675.

Caraguel, Clément. "Marivaux." *Journal des Débats* (Paris), 14 January 1860, p. 4.

Cismaru, Alfred. "Agnès and Angélique: An Attempt to Settle the Relationship." *The French Review*, 3(April 1962):472-477.

———. "*La Princesse d'Elide* in Marivaux's Theatre." *Cithara*, 3(November 1963):15-23.

———. "*Le Tartuffe* in Marivaux's Works." *Kentucky Foreign Language Quarterly*, 12(Summer 1965):142-154.

———. "*Marivaux's Les Fausses confidences*." *Cithara*, 7(November 1967):67-73.

———. "The *Moliéresque* Origins of *Les Fausses confidences*." *Kentucky Romance Quarterly*, 15(Spring 1968):223-229.

———. "*Les Sincères* and *Le Misanthrope*." *The French Review*, 42(May 1969):865-870.

———. "Molière's Influence on Marivaux's *Les Serments indiscrets*." *South Central Bulletin Studies*, 32(Winter 1972):188-199.

———. "Molière's Influence on Marivaux's *Le Père prudent et équitable*." *South Atlantic Bulletin*, 37(Spring 1973):23-28.

Courville, Xavier de. *Luigi Riccoboni dit Lélio*. Paris: Droz, 1943.

———. *Le Théâtre de Marivaux*. Paris: Le Cité des Livres, 1930.

Deloffre, Frédéric. *Marivaux et le marivaudage: Etude de langue et de style*. Paris: Les Belles Lettres, 1955.

———. *Mélanges d'histoire littéraire offerts à M. Paul Dimoff*. Paris: Annales Universitatis Saraviensis, Philosophie-Lettres, 1954.

Desboulmiers, J. A. *Histoire anecdotique et raisonnée du Théâtre Italien depuis son rétablissement en France jusqu'à l'année 1769*. Paris: Lacombe, 1769.

Donnay, Maurice. *Molière*. Paris: Arthème Fayard, 1911.

Dubuisson, Simon-Henri. *Lettres du Commissaire Dubuisson au Marquis de Caumont*. Paris: P. Arnould, 1882.

Durazzo, Comte de. *Mémoires et correspondances littéraires, dramatiques et anecdotiques*. Paris: Collin, 1808.

Fabre, Emile. *Molière*. Paris: Gallimard, 1928.

Faguet, Emile. *Dix-huitième Siècle: études littéraires*. Paris: Boivin, 1890.

Fleury, Jean. *Marivaux et le marivaudage*. Paris: Plon, 1881.

Forkey, J. *The Role of Money in French Comedy*. Baltimore: Johns Hopkins University Press, 1956.

Gautier, Théophile. *Histoire de l'art dramatique*. Paris: Magnin, Blanchard et Cie, 1858.

———. "Marivaux," *Le Moniteur universel* (Paris), 28 September 1863, p. 5.

Gazagne, Paul. *Marivaux par lui-même*. Paris: Editions du Seuil, 1954.

Gossman, Lionel. *Men and Masks: A Study of Molière*. Baltimore: The Johns Hopkins University Press, 1963.

Gossot, Emile. *Marivaux moraliste*. Paris: Didier, 1881.

Greene, E. J. H. *Marivaux*. Toronto: University of Toronto Press, 1965.

Grimm, Diderot, Raynal, Meister. *Correspondance littéraire philosophique et critique*. Paris: Garnier, 1877.

Gueullette, J. E. *Notes et souvenirs sur le Théâtre-Italien au XVIII Siècle*. Paris: E. Droz, 1938.

Hénault, Président. *Mémoires du Président Hénault écrits par lui-même*. Paris: Dentu, 1885.

Hubert, J. D. *Molière and the Comedy of Intellect*. Los Angeles: University of California Press, 1963.

Janin, J. "Les Servantes de Molière et les soubrettes de Marivaux." *Artiste*, 1(1874).

Julleville, Petit de. *Le Théâtre en France*. Paris: Nouvelle Edition, 1923.

Kemp, Robert. "*Les Sincères*." *Le Monde* (Paris), 16 September 1950, p. 23.

Kerr, Walter. *New York Herald Tribune*, 9 November 1955, p. 26.

Lafenestre, Georges. *Molière*. Paris: Hachette, 1909.

La Harpe, J. F. *Lycée, ou cours de littérature ancienne et moderne*. Paris: Hachette, 1801.

Lancaster, H. C. *French Dramatic Literature in the Seventeenth Century*. Baltimore: Johns Hopkins, 1936.

Larroumet, Gustave. *Marivaux, sa vie et ses oeuvres*. Paris: Hachette, 1881.

Le Mercure de France (Paris), 1724-1738.

Lesage, Alain René. *Oeuvres choisies*. Paris: Veuve Pissot, 1737.

Louandres, Charles. Preface in Molière, *Oeuvres*. Paris: Charles Louandres, 1885.

Lucas, Hippolyte. *Histoire du Théâtre-Français*. Paris: Charles Gosselin, 1843.

Mandel, Oscar. *Seven Comedies by Marivaux*. Ithaca, New York: Cornell University Press, 1968.

Marivaux, Pierre Carlet de. *Oeuvres complètes*. Paris: Haut-Coeur et Gayet Jeune, 1825-1830.

————. *Oeuvres complètes*. Paris: Editions Duchesne, 1881.

————. *Oeuvres complètes*. Paris: Duviquet, 1830.

————. *Théâtre complet de Marivaux*, texte établi et annoté par Jean Fournier et Maurice Bastide. Paris: Les Editions Nationales, 1946.

————. *Théâtre complet*, texte préfacé et annoté par Marcel Arland. Paris: Librairie Gallimard, 1949.

————. *Théâtre*. Paris: Editions Dort, 1961.

McKee, Kenneth N. *The Theater of Marivaux*. New York: New York University Press, 1958.

Moliere, Jean-Baptiste Poquelin. *Oeuvres*. Paris: G. Charpentier, n.d.

Nurse, P. H. "Molière précurseur de Marivaux." *Revue des sciences humaines*, n.s., fasc. 100 (1960):379-384.

————. "Marivaux et Molière." *Modern Languages*, 41(1960):102-105.

Piron, Alexis. *Oeuvres*. Paris: Duchesne, 1885.

Porte, Joseph de La. *L'Observateur littéraire*. Paris: Lambert, 1759.

Roy, Claude. *Lire Marivaux*. Paris: Editions du Seuil, 1947.

Sainte-Beuve, C. A. *Causeries du lundi*. Paris: Garnier, n.d.

Sarcey, Francisque. *Le Temps* (Paris), December 1878, p. 1.

Tilley, Arthur. *Three French Dramatists: Racine, Marivaux, Musset*. New York: Russell and Russell, 1967.

Voltaire, François-Marie Arouet. *Correspondence,* edited by Theodore Besterman. Genève: Institut et Musée Voltaire, 1953-1965.

INDEX